Culture and weight con...

Anorexia nervosa and bulimia are among the few psychiatric syndromes with a plausible sociocultural model of causation. Most books concerned with this topic have primarily considered the issues from a western perspective and have made only passing reference to other cultures. However, there is a growing body of research findings suggesting that concern with slimness is becoming more prevalent in non-western cultures and ethnicities.

In *Culture and Weight Consciousness*, Mervat Nasser brings together this research and reviews existing epidemiological and clinical work on cross-cultural aspects of eating disorders. This review is used to highlight the problematic areas in cross-cultural methodologies and to suggest directions for future research.

The author also relates the feminist theories that have been put forward to explain the phenomenon of eating disorders in the West to the condition of modern women in many non-western cultures, including the Middle East, the Far East, Africa and South America. She concludes that their position is not that different from that of their western counterparts.

Providing an informed and thought-provoking survey of eating attitudes across the world, the topical issues discussed in this book are of direct relevance to clinicians, researchers and all those interested in the links between culture, gender and health.

Mervat Nasser is a Senior Lecturer in Psychiatry at the University of Leicester and Consultant Psychiatrist, South Lincolnshire Mental Health Trust.

Culture and weight consciousness

Mervat Nasser

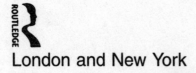

London and New York

First published 1997
by Routledge
11 New Fetter Lane, London EC4P 4EE

Simultaneously published in the USA and Canada
by Routledge
29 West 35th Street, New York, NY 10001

© 1997 Mervat Nasser

Typeset in Times by
BC Typesetting, Bristol
Printed and bound in Great Britain by
Clays Ltd., St Ives PLC

British Library Cataloguing in Publication Data
A catalogue record for this book is available from the British Library

Library of Congress Cataloging in Publication Data
Nasser, Mervat.
    Culture and weight consciousness/Mervat Nasser.
        p.   cm.
    Includes bibliographical references and index.
    1. Eating disorders–Social aspects.   2. Eating disorders–Cross
-cultural studies.   I. Title.
    RC552.E18N38   1997
    616.85′26–dc20
                                                        96-43021
                                                        CIP

ISBN 0–415–16152–5 (hbk)
        0–415–16153–3 (pbk)

For Ragai

Contents

Tables

Preface

As a medical student in Cairo university, I learnt about anorexia nervosa from the gynaecology textbook. All I knew then was that it was a rare syndrome caused by a hypothalamic disturbance and resulted in secondary amenorrhoea. I could not have envisaged, however, that one day I would be heavily involved with the subject to the extent of writing a book on it.

My limited knowledge then was not the result of any shortcomings in my medical education; the condition of anorexia nervosa was considered in all medical literature at that time as a rare phenomenon. It is true to say that the expansion of our knowledge on this topic took place only in the past two decades.

The interesting thing, however, has been the shift in our understanding of this peculiar and enigmatic condition, from a rare syndrome caused by some sort of brain pathology to a product of forces within society. It is now generally accepted that the main contribution to the development of this disorder comes from the patient's own sociocultural environment. This new insight was derived mainly from the bulk of epidemiological research that pointed to an increase in the incidence of these disorders in recent times and showed them to occur in varying degrees of severity in normal populations.

The phenomenon was linked to changes in aesthetic standards, with an increased tendency towards the idealization of thinness. These new ideals were promoted through the media and the fashion industry. Thinness became equated with beauty, achievement and success. The disorder also occurred overwhelmingly in women, which made feminist writers speculate on the possible relationship between the predicament of the modern woman, and this new syndrome. Thinness was seen as a metaphor combining desirable qualities of the new woman, namely control, with the qualities required from the traditional woman, i.e. attractiveness, weakness and helplessness.

A relevant observation was the fact that all reports of this condition appeared to be emerging from western industrialized countries, mainly western Europe, Canada and North America. The syndrome was unreported or under-reported in other countries and cultures. This gave rise to the notion that the syndrome was unique to western culture. This was supported by what were perceived as differences in aesthetic standards between West and non-West, besides other factors including differentials of wealth. This was the angle that attracted me most to the subject; I have always seen myself as a psychiatrist with particular interest in social and cultural issues.

It began in 1980 when I was a registrar at the Royal Free Hospital, London. In one of the journal club sessions, I was responsible for presenting a paper that had just been published by two Canadian research workers, David Garner and Paul Garfinkel, demonstrating that ballerinas were at considerable risk of developing anorexia nervosa because of pressures imposed on them to be thin for career reasons. Two things happened at that meeting: the first was a point made by one of the audience, who questioned why music students, who were among the groups studied, did not show the same vulnerability to this disorder as the ballet students, despite the fact that they were equally delicate – as if anorexia nervosa was a privilege or a measure of one's degree of sophistication! The other was a remark made by one of my colleagues, who said 'I suppose it would have been different if they were belly dancers!'

The last comment made me see the value of applying all these observations and stereotyped assumptions to scientific testing. I was aware that thinness was not strongly overvalued in my own culture, and in certain social classes plumpness or even obesity was thought to be desirable. However, obesity was not at any time regarded positively by middle-class families and was, on the whole, less of a problem in the past than it is now. Any recent increase in the rates of obesity in Egyptian society has been associated simultaneously with a steady increase in weight consciousness.

An increase in weight consciousness against a background of general weight gain was a personal experience for me after I came to England. Weight was one of a range of issues of which I suddenly became conscious, like being a foreigner and a career woman. For some reason I naively assumed that all women in Britain were in paid work! I also became aware of how career ambitions for women could be seen as unnatural, an issue that hardly crossed my mind when I was in Egypt. This was highlighted through an encounter with a British white female medical student who was in real distress after she passed her psychiatry final examinations with distinction. She thought that her success could be at the expense of her popularity. The concept that success and popularity for a woman do not go together was a difficult concept for me to grasp. And yet, I thought, who should care about popularity who is indeed successful; perhaps my own competitiveness was more natural to me than it was for her.

The difference between us on the issues of success and popularity for women was rather surprising given the general assumptions that are held about the position of women in our respective cultures. Obviously, neither of us could be seen as representative of our own cultures, but these differences can still be viewed as reflecting different cultural notions. At this stage, however, I had no idea of what culture really meant; the complexities of the concept baffled me then and continue to baffle me. All I could say was that as an Egyptian child the first book I read in my life was an Arabic translation of *Robinson Crusoe*! If you have started to wonder about the relationship between *Robinson Crusoe* and eating disorders, wait until you have read the last chapter of this book.

Fired with enthusiasm, I began to think of the best way to contemplate the question of whether anorexia nervosa does exist in Arabic culture or not. I started first by screening all the referrals to the Royal Free anorexia nervosa unit, to find if they included Arab nationals. I did not find any, although the Royal Free catchment area normally attracts Arab patients.

The only other course of action was to conduct a community study on Arab nationals living in the UK. I am greatly indebted to Professor Anthony Wakeling for encouraging me to embark on this study. I registered the subject for an M Phil degree with London University and I was fortunate to have Professor Anthony Mann as my supervisor, to whom I will always remain grateful.

The plan was to compare two groups of Arab students: one attending London University, and a comparable group of students at Cairo University. The objective was to see if the London group would prove to be more vulnerable to the development of eating pathology by reasons of its exposure to British cultural norms in relation to weight and feminine beauty.

The design of the study may appear very simple but in reality I had to face several problems – mainly the absence at that time of any literature on the subject and the lack of any previous studies. The major difficulty, however, was the recruitment of a sufficiently large sample of Arab female students in London, as Arab students, particularly females, were then a rather rare commodity.

I approached London University faculties, particularly the School of Oriental and African Studies, the London School of Economics and others. My difficulty was compounded by the absence of records of ethnicity, which meant that I had to identify the group by their names and meet each one individually. Obviously the group was a selective one, but that was through necessity not choice. All the Arab female students I could identify at the time were included, and the Cairo group had to be matched very closely with it.

The results of this study came as a real surprise. A significant proportion of the London group showed concern about weight similar to that found in high-risk groups in the West, almost approaching the percentage found in the Garner and Garfinkel study on ballet students.

The findings of the study were presented at the International Conference on Eating Disorders at Swansea in 1984, and were well received. This conference was a turning point in my life. I met figures who had made valuable contributions in the field of eating disorders research and others who have, over the course of time, enriched our understanding of the nature of these disorders. The first was Professor Gerald Russell whose school of thought and diagnostic model I adhered to in my research. I met Professor Sten Theander of Sweden who was the first to point to an increase in the incidence of anorexia nervosa and has been particularly interested in my work since then. I met Professor David Garner who was complimentary of my study which used the Eating Attitude Test questionnaire for the first time on a non-western population. The EAT has since been translated into a number of different languages and used extensively in this type of research. I met Professor Joseph Silverman who participated in an early study that showed ballerinas to be at risk of anorexia nervosa. He came to me after the presentation and said 'You have started a life time's work'. He was right!

I also met Richard Gordon, whose book *Anorexia and Bulimia: An Anatomy of a Social Epidemic* is referred to several times in the course of this book, and Hans Hook of the Netherlands who has recently shown in collaboration with his colleagues the impact of urbanization on the rates of eating disorders – an aspect I believe will have great relevance to all concerned with sociocultural research in this field. All the people I mentioned have been particularly kind to me, have shared their thoughts with me and have continued to show an interest in my work over the years.

This positive response was not universally shared. Some, understandably, challenged the work and doubted certain aspects of its validity, based on clear methodological issues. The other reasons for their doubt were perhaps related more to the fact that the study was conducted in a society like Egypt, a society that has a developing economy and is perceived by many as remote from western culture.

Part of the scepticism could be justified in the context that people like myself are hardly represented in the western media. It is almost guaranteed that the cover of any current travel book on Egypt will still have a picture of a camel or a peasant. This is not to say that camels and peasants do not exist in Egypt, but it also contains millions of graduates from Egyptian universities, nearly half of them women.

This made me more aware than ever of the need to confront the issue of culture, and when the study was later replicated to form the basis of my doctorate, I attempted to explore the issue of culture in more depth. Some of the aspects of my argument were presented at the European Congress on Eating Disorders (ECED) meeting in Prague 1993, where the title of my paper was 'The vague vocabulary of transcultural research'; a great deal of it is covered in the last chapter of this book. The paper was presented against a background of increased information emanating from different societies, particularly eastern Europe, indicating that eating disorders are on the increase after the recent political changes.

It may sound rather wild to make a connection between eating disorders and communism. And yet it is true to say that this is more or less the main line of my argument, which stresses the importance of the existing economic system in the making or shaping of cultures. It also highlights how the position and the perception of women's roles can alter with a change in the politico-economic system.

The argument interested those who felt, like me, a strong need to refine our approach to transcultural research. Gunther Rathner has recently started, with colleagues in other centres in Europe, to look methodically at differences in the magnitude of eating pathology in eastern Europe following the political changes and the subsequent economic transformation of the 1990s.

The recent increase in publications from centres across the world dealing with the prevalence of eating disorders in their cultures has highlighted the need for this book. My purpose is primarily to gather this published material in a coherent manner for the benefit of future research. I also hope that through the book I will be able to express my own views about what I believe is happening with cultures today and challenge some of the accepted beliefs that are held about non-western societies. The world in my opinion is increasingly subscribing to universal media icons and opting for similar economic systems, and yet continues to see itself as diverse and pluralistic.

The first chapter of the book deals with the factors that historically led to the evolution of the thinness ideal, with the relationship between dieting behaviour and eating pathology and with all the other evidence that supports the argument for the sociocultural causation of eating disorders.

In the second chapter, the concept of whether eating disorders are culture bound or not is re-examined. Eating disorders have long been considered specific to western culture, and it is true that these syndromes cannot be fully understood outside the context of culture. There is sufficient evidence, however, to show that these disorders are no longer unique to one particular culture. Weight consciousness has clearly spread to other cultures subsequent to the process of globalization.

The third chapter aims to offer a systematic review of the research published in this area and provides possible explanations for the results. This review includes case reports of eating disorders among ethnic groups in the USA and the UK, prevalence and comparative prevalence studies from Japan, the Middle East, China, India, South America and Africa. It also draws attention to the recent intra-European variations with reference to post-communist eastern Europe. The results are explained in terms of changes in dietary habits, a worldwide increase in the prevalence of obesity, interfamilial and intergenerational conflicts, migrational stress, as well as the role of the media.

In the fourth chapter, I deal with the issue of the vulnerability of 'other women' to eating pathology. Feminist theories that were put forward to explain the increased propensity of women in the West to eating disorders are examined in connection with women in non-western countries. The focus in this part of the book is on 'feminism across cultures'. Attention is given to the condition of modern women in these societies, and it is argued that their position is not all that different from their western counterparts.

The last chapter of the book addresses the current limitations of the concept of culture. This critique has implications for future transcultural research, as it forces the whole doctrine to examine its current terminology and methodology with reference to the West/non-West dichotomy. There is now growing evidence to show that the young, middle-class and educated share common concerns that transcend national boundaries and presumed cultural differences. The book is intended to raise the profile of this important issue to form the basis for further research and provoke more fruitful debate.

In the preparation of this book I benefited from discussions with several members of the ECED, particularly Bridget Dolan and Gunther Rathner. I was also helped by a number of people to whom I am very grateful. Special thanks are due to my secretary Jaqui Harris for her sincerity, genuine understanding and her willingness to help in any way she can to make my task easier. I would also like to thank my academic secretary Irene Chenery for her general support and specifically for checking the bibliography of this book. I am indebted to Helena Swartifigure for her enormous help with the literature search, and also to Gweneth Strachan and Sheila Stevenson for swiftly requesting some of the literature I needed.

Finally I would like to thank my husband Ragai Shaban, without whose tolerance and unlimited support this book would not have been possible.

Mervat Nasser
Leicester, 1996

Abbreviations

The following abbreviations are used in journal titles in the Bibliography

Abnorm.	Abnormal
Acad.	Academy
Adolesc.	Adolescent
Am.	American
Ann.	Annals (of)
Arch.	Archives
Assoc.	Association
Aust.	Australia(n)
Behav.	Behaviour(al)
Br.	British
Bull.	Bulletin
Clin.	Clinical
Cult.	Cultural
Dis.	Disease(s)
Disord.	Disorders
Epidemiol.	Epidemiology
Eur.	European
Exp.	Experimental
Gen.	General
Hist.	History
Hosp.	Hospital
Int.	International
J.	Journal
Jpn.	Japan(ese)
Med.	Medicine/Medical
Ment.	Mental

Monogr.	Monograph(s)
Neurolog.	Neurology/Neurological
Nrv.	Nervous
Paed.	Paediatrics
Proc.	Proceedings
Psychiat.	Psychiatry/Psychiatric/Psychiatrica
Psychoanal.	Psychoanalysis/Psychoanalytical
Psychol.	Psychology/Psychological
Quart.	Quarterly
Rep.	Reports
Res.	Research
Rev.	Review
Roy.	Royal
Scand.	Scandinavia(n)
Sci.	Science
Soc.	Social/Society (of)
Sociol.	Sociology/Sociological
Ther.	Therapy

Now the trouble with the idea of culture is that it entails not only venerating one's own culture but also thinking of it as somehow divorced from – because transcending – the everyday world.
Edward Said, Culture and Imperialism

Chapter 1

The sociocultural model of eating pathology

WEIGHT CONSCIOUSNESS AND THE PURSUIT OF THINNESS

Weight phobia, fear of fatness and pursuit of thinness are modern terms that are now used interchangeably to refer to anorexia nervosa, a condition that was first reported in the latter part of the nineteenth century by William Gull in Britain and Charles Lasègue in France. Both described a distinct state of self starvation, peculiar to young women and likely to be caused by a host of emotional factors.

Implicit in their description is the presence of concern over weight and a desire to be thin. Lasègue was intrigued by the patient's indifference to her thinness and her total acceptance of her weight loss.

> What dominates the mental condition of the patient is above all a state of quietude, I might also say a condition of contentment purely pathological. . . . Not only does she not sigh for recovery but she is not ill pleased with her condition.
>
> (Lasègue 1873)

It could not have been a simple coincidence that at the time of describing this syndrome, both London and Paris were witnessing their first feminist movement. Contemporary feminist writers viewed thinness as a way of resolving the modern woman's inner conflict, torn between a desire to conform to old traditional stereotypes of womanhood and the new values related to what the modern woman ought to be. It has been argued that in our century the thinness ideal has evolved as the ultimate metaphor, representing a perfect synthesis of the old notions of attractiveness, frailty and fashionability that women are still expected to have and the new values of autonomy, achievement and self-control (Orbach 1986, Wolf 1990, Gordon 1990).

The debate about whether thinness has indeed provided women with an answer to their current predicament is an important aspect of this book and will be dealt with in more detail later on. However, the cult of thinness has historically evolved for a number of other reasons, some of which could perhaps be seen as being directly or indirectly connected with the position of women in our society today.

In the nineteenth century, for instance, thinness began to be positively perceived as representing a kind of spiritual beauty. This is clearly seen in the romanticization of the thin, tubercular look in literature and poetry. TB was believed to affect only sensitive people and enhance their creative power. Gautier, one of the leaders of the romantic movement, commented that he could not have accepted as a lyrical poet any one weighing more than 99 pounds! Shelley consoled Keats by saying that consumption was a disease fond of people who wrote good verses. Byron, too, starved himself to unnatural thinness and wished to die from consumption 'because the ladies would say, look at the poet Byron, how interesting he looks in dying' (cited in Sontag 1978). The fashion of looking consumptive and pale was taken up by some women, who used whitening powder to achieve it (Vincent 1979).

It is interesting that, at that time, physicians had to be aware of the distinction between this emerging new syndrome of anorexia nervosa and the more familiar condition of consumption. Interest in comparison of the two conditions has not disappeared; questions have recently been raised as to whether some of the past romantic literary figures had TB or anorexia nervosa (Dally 1989, Frank 1990).

Art provided another platform for the expression of society's new aesthetic values, with notable departure from the fuller and sensuous figures of Rubens and Renoir to the dream-like women of the Pre-Raphaelites. The ultimate endorsement of thinness as the new form of beauty was through Picasso's painting, the *Girl in Chemise*, where, according to Clark (1980), 'A new beauty has emerged, withdrawn, melancholic, delicate and frail'. The fashion industry was ready to capitalize on this new look and promote the thinner image: 'An abundance of fat', said Helena Rubinstein, 'is not in accord with the principles that rule our conception of the beautiful' (Rubinstein 1930).

The change in aesthetic values, with more admiration given to the thinner female figure, was initially endorsed by the rich, who were able to purchase this fashionable look; this is epitomized in the often-quoted saying by the Duchess of Windsor, 'One cannot be too rich . . . one cannot be too thin'.

The class structure of society was changing significantly towards the end of the nineteenth century, with the rise of the middle class. Lasègue (1873) was clever enough to make the link between his new syndrome *L'anorexie hystérique* and the changes that were happening in middle-class families, with increased emphasis on eating and appearance. Eating emerged as a new style that set the members of the middle class apart from the working class, and meal times began to symbolize the spirit and values of these new middle-class families (Brumberg 1988, Selvini-Palazzoli 1985).

It is not surprising therefore that attention was given to the subject of class and weight; an inverse relationship between socio-economic class and prevalence of obesity has often been reported (Goldblatt *et al.* 1965, Sobal and Stunkard 1989). In keeping with the class symbolism of thinness, early literature on anorexia nervosa showed an over-representation of these disorders among patients from upper socio-economic classes (Crisp 1970, Bruch 1973, Morgan and Russell 1975).

The glamorization of thinness in fashion was to spread throughout society on account of the ready-to-wear industry's investment in this smaller and thinner look through the introduction of standard sizing for all women (Walsh 1979, Shorter 1984). It was predicted that as fashion became increasingly more accessible to women from different class backgrounds, a rise in the proportion of patients with anorexia nervosa from lower socio-economic classes would be expected (Garfinkel *et al.* 1980).

The historical evolution of the thin look and the role played by the fashion industry and the media in propagating this idealized image have been the subject of a number of publications in recent years (Schwartz 1986, Brumberg 1988, Gordon 1990). Advertisements on slimness targeted towards women were shown to have grown dramatically more numerous in the past two decades (Garner and Garfinkel 1980, Schwarz *et al.* 1986, Anderson and Di Domenico 1992). Also the number of diet articles and diet books increased significantly. The most influential has been the

Beverly Hills diet, which according to Wooley and Wooley (1982), represents the mass marketing of anorexia nervosa: 'Anorexia nervosa has been marketed as a cure for obesity . . . the popularity of this diet can be seen as yet another symptom of a weight obsessed culture'.

As a result, more women than men began to show higher levels of body dissatisfaction. Women were consistently found to view themselves larger than their real shape and the shape they think men prefer. Interestingly too, men were also found to prefer women to be thinner than the women felt themselves to be, indicating that the preference for a thinner body shape for women is shared by both sexes (Fallon and Rozin 1985). This explains the results of the studies that looked at the prevalence of dieting behaviour, which showed more women than men to be commonly engaged in dieting. Dieting behaviour was found to be prevalent in 50–80 per cent of younger women, who repeatedly described themselves as being overweight and reported an exaggerated concern with their weight (Dwyer et al. 1969, Nylander 1971, Moses et al. 1989, Rand and Kuldau 1991).

One of the reasons for the high susceptibility of young people to dieting is the fact that they develop early in life a negative attitude towards obesity, concomitant with increased awareness of the stigma attached to it in society (Wooley et al. 1979). The negative attitude towards obesity partly stems from the recognition of the possible health risks associated with it. Obesity was linked to a wide variety of diseases, particularly hypertension and heart conditions; even early mortality was also attributed to it. The link between obesity and heart diseases still dominates medical thought and is regarded by the lay public as a health fact, despite some medical publications questioning this relationship and warning against interpreting correlation figures as indicative of definite causality (Mann 1975).

Coinciding with the trend in fashion towards a thinner body shape, the medical establishment started to pay a lot of attention to body weight, with the introduction of weight charts and standard body weights for heights. Weighing the patient became routine and standard procedure in all medical examinations (Brumberg 1988). This contributed to the growing obsession with fitness. Thinness and fitness are closely linked and exercising through such activities as jogging and aerobics have become common preoccupations. Overexercising was found to occur in

18 per cent of the American population, and 30 per cent of those aged 18 to 24 reported regular jogging. The level of jogging per week was found to be directly linked to involvement with dieting (Richert and Hummers 1986).

All of this meant more pressure being put on women to pursue thinness, as thinness not only offered beauty but also became increasingly synonymous with the healthy younger look that everyone desired.

It is ironic that this heightened weight consciousness and the rise in society's expectation of thinness took place against an increase in population weight norms, particularly for women (Garner *et al.* 1980). Women are biologically more prone to weight gain than men; a woman has twice as much fat as the male and an increase in body fat is expected to take place around significant times in the female life cycle, i.e. puberty, pregnancy, and menopause. Women also have a lower metabolic rate than men which increases their difficulty in reducing their weight through dieting. Dieting in itself is known to lower the metabolic rate even further, thus initiating the familiar cycle of repeated frustration through unsuccessful dieting that a lot of women experience (Bray 1976, Bennett and Gurin 1982).

It has been argued, however, that the pursuit of thinness is not only about the cult of appearance; it is more indicative of the competitive spirit that pervades our time: 'Of importance here is the pressure on women to be competitive and successful; these achievement pressures may force an adolescent girl into a position where weight control becomes equal to self control and success' (Garner and Garfinkel 1979).

Slade (1982) proposed that the stress generated by insecurities about adult roles could drive the potential anorexic to seek thinness as a source of achievement and success. Women were found to be easily manipulated into thinking that their body image was a measure of their value and sense of achievement and control, with success and self-worth equating to a desirable body shape (Bruch 1978).

If dieting is successful, the woman's behaviour is reinforced by the weight loss. The more competitive the environment, the stronger the environmental reinforcers (Garner *et al.* 1980). On the other hand, excessive dieting behaviour could also be successfully brought under control in the absence of these environmental reinforcers (Szmukler *et al.* 1985).

Thinness is not only seen as a measure of success, but also sometimes as a licence to succeed. Overweight individuals were more likely to be discriminated against in educational and vocational settings than thinner ones. The commonest form of prejudice was clearly found to be targeted towards women who are perceived as having typically feminine bodies as reflected in bust/waist ratios. These women are commonly seen as less academically inclined and possibly less competent professionally (Canning and Meyer 1966, Larkin and Pines 1979, Cash and Janda 1984).

In view of all this, some women had no choice but to identify with the thinness ideal which would not only render them more beautiful and attractive but could also provide them with an important credential for success and professional enhancement.

FROM DIETING TO EATING DISORDERS

The symptoms of eating disorders clearly revolve around fear of fatness and a strong desire to be thin. These symptoms can easily be seen as extensions of culturally acceptable behaviours and preoccupations. However, the boundary between formal eating pathology and the more prevalent dieting behaviour is far from clear and is the subject of continuing debate.

Russell (1979) considered the dread of fatness to be the essence of eating disorders, but Palmer (1993) argued against using weight concern as the defining issue in these disorders. In support of Russell's argument, those engaged in obsessional dieting were found to have the potential risk of developing eating disorders at a later stage (King 1989). Within the course of one year, the dieters among adolescent schoolgirls were found to have an eightfold increased risk of developing an eating disorder (Patton 1988). Body dissatisfaction was also shown to be a significant predictive factor for the later development of the full syndromes (Garfinkel et al. 1992).

The main source of support for the link between dieting and eating disorders did in fact emerge from community surveys that looked for the prevalence of these disorders among normal student populations. This age group was repeatedly found to be concerned with dieting and was subsequently considered most at risk of developing eating disorders. It was also thought that the spirit of achievement that pervades academic establishments could increase the risk in this group. The morbid concern with weight was measured by a positive response on the Eating Attitude Test questionnaire (EAT). The EAT is a self-report questionnaire that was devised to elicit abnormalities in eating attitudes and measure a broad range of symptoms characteristic of anorexia nervosa (Garner and Garfinkel 1979). The concern over these issues ranged in these student populations between 6.3 and 11 per cent. On clinical interviewing, 2–5 per cent of the students were found to have a partial syndrome of an eating disorder, manifesting with morbid concerns over food and body weight that were nonetheless not severe enough to qualify for the diagnosis of the full syndrome (Button and Whitehouse 1981, Clarke and Palmer 1983, Szmukler 1983, Mann et al. 1983, Johnson-Sabine et al. 1988).

Subclinical forms of eating pathology were generally estimated to be five times more common than the full-blown syndromes (Dancyger and Garfinkel 1995). The actual presence of these subclinical forms and the frequency of their occurrence clearly suggest that eating pathology behaves on a continuum of severity, with dieting representing one end of the spectrum and the extreme forms of disordered eating representing the other.

Dieting was therefore considered to be a necessary if not sufficient factor for the development of the full syndrome. The question that remains largely unresolved is what determines the progression of a partial syndrome into a definite clinical case. Doubts were raised as to the degree of similarity in the psychological profile between those with partial syndrome and those with a definite eating disorder (Bunnell et al. 1990). Other studies showed them to be comparable in the level of their psychological disturbance with particular reference to the presence of anxiety and depression (Garfinkel et al. 1995).

In view of these reservations it was important still not to put all the emphasis on the dieting behaviour alone but to take also into account the individual's other vulnerabilities, particularly psychosocial functioning, as the nature of the eating disorder lies more in the entanglement of the dietary restraint and its consequences with a variety of wider personal issues (Palmer 1993, Dancyger and Garfinkel 1995).

The discovery of subclinical cases in student populations encouraged interest in studying other populations that are not necessarily designated as being at risk of developing eating disorders. Studies conducted on general practice population showed similar levels of concern, and the significant finding was once again the presence of a higher number of those with partial syndromes as opposed to those with full eating disorders syndrome with a tendency to develop bulimia nervosa (Meadows *et al.* 1986, King 1986).

A close relationship was in fact found between dieting behaviour and bulimic symptoms, which tend to develop within a year from the onset of dieting, particularly in women who have poor impulse control. Purging was also found to be more prevalent among adolescents than originally thought, and it was suggested that it should be considered an early stage in the development of the full bulimic syndrome (Polivy *et al.* 1994, Killen *et al.* 1985).

The finding of greater prevalence of bulimia than anorexia nervosa in community studies contradicted the original assumptions held about the nature of the bulimic syndrome. The term bulimia was introduced by Russell to refer to a variant of anorexia nervosa that is possibly more sinister and could have poorer outcome. Russell's description was based on the observation that nearly half of his anorexic population exhibited symptoms of binge eating following periods of self-starvation (Russell 1979).

Binge eating was initially considered to be synonymous with bulimia. Binge eating was found to be a fairly common behaviour which was not necessarily interpreted as evidence of pathology (Palmer 1983). The focus on binge eating created discrepancies in research findings, particularly between US and UK studies, where the reported prevalence of bulimia in the community ranged between 1 and 19 per cent (Halmi *et al.* 1981, Cooper and Fairburn 1983, Pyle *et al.* 1983, Katzman *et al.* 1984, Healy *et al.* 1985, Herzog *et al.* 1986, Howat and Saxton 1988, King 1989).

Notwithstanding variations in diagnostic practices, and indeed any possible underlying cultural differences, between British and US societies, these relatively high rates of bulimia in normal population studies clearly suggested that bulimia and not anorexia nervosa is the commonest form of eating disorder.

One explanation for the spread of bulimia is that purging and vomiting are seen as perhaps more successful means of controlling weight than is dieting. The individual can engage in normal if not excessive eating and still keep weight within desired limits. Those who have bulimia are often not thin enough to attract attention, and amenorrhoea, a diagnostic feature in anorexia nervosa, is also unusual. These are the features that make the bulimic disorder harder to identify.

Bulimia was also found to be easily mimicked to the extent that it can be considered a socially contagious behaviour. Women's magazines and the media have been claimed to be responsible for increasing awareness of the existence of bulimic behaviours, which may have helped to spread them. When an advertisement was placed in *Cosmopolitan* magazine requesting people who use self-induced vomiting as a method of controlling their weight to come forward, 83 per cent of the respondents were considered to have met the criteria for bulimia nervosa. When similar work was done again, using on this occasion a television program, 63 per cent were regarded as having bulimia nervosa. These high rates raised the suspicion that the publicity surrounding these behaviours could be a factor in popularizing them (Cooper and Fairburn 1982, 1984, Chiodo and Latimer 1983, Lawrence 1984).

Both anorexia and bulimia nervosa were subsumed under 'eating disorders' – a term that was introduced to acknowledge the full spectrum of eating pathology. This concept has been incorporated in both the *American Diagnostic Manual* (DSM1V) and the *International Classification of Mental and Behavioural Disorders* (ICD10). Russell (1985) maintained that the concept of eating disorders implied an interrelated set of disorders with several underlying features, the most important being *the morbid fear of becoming fat and the desire to be thin.*

Since weight consciousness is regarded as the phenomenon underpinning eating disorders, it would be logical to expect that these disorders should be overrepresented in certain groups where conformity to thinness is considered a prerequisite for career success.

It has long been recognized that certain populations by reasons of career choice must focus increased attention on, and control over, their body shape: such as professional dancers, models and athletes. In the description of Pavlova, by Agnes de Mille, this celebration of thinness is clearly seen: 'There was not an ounce of spare flesh on her skeleton and the life force used and used her body until she died of fever of moving, gasping for breath . . . her look was small and strapped of all anatomy' (cited in Vincent 1979).

Research showed ballerinas to have disturbed body image similar to that of the anorexic population. They were shown to engage in excessive dieting, overexercise and occasionally vomiting as a way of controlling their weight (Druss and Silverman 1979).

Ballet and modelling students were the subject of a major, influential study that contributed greatly to our understanding of the sociocultural factors that may cause eating disorders. Thirty per cent of the ballet and modelling students studied scored positively on the Eating Attitude Test questionnaire. Significantly, all were reported to have developed their anorexic tendencies after starting their training. Nearly 7 per cent of the sample met the criteria for a full syndrome of anorexia nervosa. This high percentage highlighted the risks involved in this career (Garner and Garfinkel 1980). The pressures to slim were found to be endemic in ballet schools and was also related to the degree of competitiveness in the environment. The more competitive the environment, the more likely was it that weight loss would be positively encouraged and reinforced (Szmukler *et al.* 1985).

The pressure to be thin even put men at risk of developing abnormal eating behaviours. Male racing jockeys were found to be under similar pressures to those affecting ballerinas and models. Trainees in this field regard low weight as crucial to success; their need to maintain a low weight, together with the knowledge of the methods of weight reduction, are integral parts of horse racing culture. A high percentage of abnormal eating behaviours, as measured by positive scores on the Eating Attitude Test questionnaire, were found in this population. The methods used by the jockeys to control their weight greatly resembled those found in the clinical group of anorexics and bulimics and included the use of laxatives, diuretics and self-induced vomiting (King and Mezey 1987).

The relationship between athleticism and eating disorders has attracted more interest in recent years, to the extent that the term *anorexia athletica* has been proposed. A significant proportion of athletes were found to suffer eating disorders, particularly if they were competing in sports in which leanness or specific weight were required (Imm and Pruitt 1991, Sundgot-Borgen 1993). The issue of competitiveness in sport was raised again alongside the emphasis on thinness, the higher the degree of competitiveness the more the risk. This was demonstrated in the case of competitive runners who were shown to exhibit similar physical and psychological features to those of anorexia nervosa sufferers (Weight and Noakes 1987).

The cultural preoccupation with thinness and the spread of dieting have all been reflected in the historical progress of the prevalence of the full syndromes of eating disorders. Despite the fact that anorexia nervosa was described in the latter part of the nineteenth century, it has only achieved prominence in psychiatric literature in the past thirty years. The subject of anorexia nervosa and eating pathology in general became the focus of much interest and academic investigation, reflected in the rise of the number of professional bodies specializing in eating disorders research and treatment. This rise in interest has been in part a direct result of a perceived rise in the incidence of these disorders. Anorexia nervosa, which was once considered rare, began to be referred to as a social epidemic (Bruch 1978, Gordon 1990).

The impression that anorexia nervosa was on the increase was confirmed by research that calculated the number of cases presented to medical attention over a period of time. Naturally these data were expected to be an underestimate as they only relied on diagnosed cases that actively sought medical help. In spite of this limitation the majority of these studies still showed a steady increase in the incidence of this disorder (Kendell *et al.* 1973, Duddle 1973, Szmukler *et al.* 1984). In Sweden, Theander (1970) was able to demonstrate an increase in hospitalized cases over a thirty-year period. Other studies of hospital records showed evidence of a rise of 80 per cent and 150 per cent over a period of two decades in the USA and Scotland (Jones *et al.* 1980).

Some argued that the increase in new cases does not in fact reflect a genuine increase in these disorders as much as it shows a general improvement in recognizing them and a tendency to report them more often. In addition, there is evidence of a recent demographic change in the general population whereby the proportion of young women who are known to be at risk of developing this disorder is increasing (Williams and King 1987).

Despite all reservations, the evidence from recent research confirms a genuine increase in the occurrence of eating pathology over the past fifty years (Lucas *et al.* 1991, Hoek 1993).

Recently, attention was drawn to yet another important piece of epidemiological evidence in support of this sociocultural model of causation: namely, the presence of intracultural variations in the incidence of these disorders in any society. More interest is now given to the issue of urbanization and its impact on the prevalence of eating pathology. Despite the scarcity of available studies that attempted to explore this issue, the emerging evidence points to possible urban/rural differences in the rates of eating disorders.

In Japan, for instance, the incidence of anorexia nervosa was found to be one in two thousand in rural areas compared with one in five hundred in urban areas. This finding was confirmed again in another Japanese study, where the incidence of anorexia nervosa was three times higher in densely populated areas (Azuma and Henmi 1982, Ohezeki *et al.* 1990). The level of urbanization in the Netherlands was shown to increase the risk of developing bulimia nervosa (Hoek *et al.* 1995). However the prevalence rates for eating disorders in the Austrian Tyrol and rural Italy were found to be comparable to those in other European cities (Rathner and Messner 1993). The apparent association between the occurrence of these syndromes and the level of urbanization is an exciting new development that awaits further study and investigation.

So, it is clear that the argument for sociocultural causation of eating disorders derives its strength from cultural, subcultural and intra-cultural determinants (see Table 1.1). The increase in the incidence of these disorders over the latter half of this century has been linked to the great cultural value placed on thinness. Women have subscribed to the thinness ideal for all the positive

Table 1.1 Eating disorders – the sociocultural model

Nature of psychopathology	Symbolic of notions of thinness cherished and promoted by culture Positive stereotypes ascribed to thinness (beauty, health, class, success) Merges with the normal dieting behaviour
Gender specific	An answer to the 'modern woman dilemma': torn between conflicting/ contradictory roles
The epidemiologic evidence	A steady increase over the past 50 years Behaves on a spectrum of severity; evidence of subclinical forms The spread of bulimia; ? socially contagious
Sub-cultural variations	More prevalent in certain groups where thinness is endemic (ballerinas, models, athletes)
Intracultural variations	Higher prevalence in urban than rural areas
Cross-cultural variations	Culture specific/bound; ? unique to western culture

attributes ascribed to it. Thinness nowadays symbolizes beauty, attractiveness, fashionability, health, achievement, and control. The emphasis on dieting and the demand for thinness is highlighted in certain subcultures like those of dancers, models and athletes, who have been found to be more at risk of developing eating disorders by reason of their career demands. There is also another possible risk linked to the level of urbanization: the more urbanized the society the more likely that these disorders will prevail.

However, one of the important aspects of this argument has always been the apparent transcultural variation whereby these disorders have been considered rare or, indeed, absent in non-western societies; this made some regard eating disorders as a phenomenon unique to western culture. The exploration of this particular aspect of the sociocultural argument is the focus of this book.

Chapter 2

The concept of culture boundedness and eating disorders

THE DEFINITION OF A CULTURE-BOUND SYNDROME

The term 'culture-bound syndrome' was coined by Yap (1951) and refers to a collection of signs and symptoms which is not to be found universally in human populations, but is restricted to a particular culture or group of cultures.

Despite the clarity of this definition, the understanding of what we consider as culture-bound syndromes is far from simple. It depends entirely on the school of thought to which one is prepared to subscribe. There are mainly two approaches to this problem; each has its proponents and decibels and neither is without contentions.

The first approach is the *generalist* which is derived from Emil Kraepelin's (1904) writings on the subject. It is commonly referred to as the traditional transcultural school of thought, one that considers culture-bound syndromes as atypical or variant presentations of an accepted and recognized pathology (Kiev 1972). In that context a culture-bound syndrome is an exotic phenomenon that affects *other* people. The familiar reports of culture-bound syndromes often have certain eccentric qualities ascribed to them and include rather unusual conditions like Amok (homicidal tendency to be found in south east Asia), Latah (trance-like states common to women in the south Pacific) and Koro (the delusion of the receding penis).

All of these conditions were seen as local reactions, which if assessed properly need not be assigned a diagnosis independent from the classic psychiatric diagnostic framework. In this approach, 'culture' is considered of importance only in shaping the final presentation of the disorder, i.e. it is *pathoplastic*. Proponents of this approach clearly dispute the argument that within any culture there are elements that are necessary and sufficient to have a causative force: 'To date no psychiatric condition has been identified that is peculiar to one culture' (Leff 1988).

Whilst this may be true of conditions that are now recognized to have neurobiological basis, the attempt to make all culture-bound disorders conform to one and only one diagnostic system that has been developed in the West, was seen by some as undermining some unique and powerful features of other cultures and dictating to others western modes of thinking, hence re-enforcing the supremacy of western culture.

The second is the *culture-specific*, or the meaning-centred approach, which evolved through medical anthropology. Within this framework, differences within societies are emphasized. These differences concern variable ways of perceiving and conceptualizing the world. The main proponent of the meaning-centred approach is Kleinman (1977). His premise is based on the relativity of both normality and abnormality, which in his opinion can only be defined within the social and cultural context. This approach examines the mind through shared cultural categories and focuses on the relationship between public and private symbolism and how the individual makes sense of his own personal situation (Littlewood 1984).

The Kleinmanian approach is not concerned with whether culture-bound syndromes are similar to other mainstream psychiatric categories or not; instead it tends to see these syndromes in terms of specific cultural preoccupations and the meaning they impart. This approach is an interpretative one that searches for explanatory models for the disorders within cultures.

Attributing an explanatory or causative force to cultures implies that cultures are *pathogenic*. This notion of cultural causality is embedded in Ritenbaugh's (1982) model which is also shared by Cassidy (1982). In their view a culture-specific disorder cannot be understood apart from its specific cultural or subcultural context and its aetiology symbolizes core meanings and behaviours that are considered norms of that culture.

This approach does not tell us, however, how any cultural text is written and how the so-called shared cultural categories are defined. It is difficult to know on what basis an objective assessment can be made of a highly subjective cultural value system.

The inclusion of notions of causation as supportive of cultural specificity has the problem of increasing the vagueness of the concept, since any notions of cause are variable and constantly changing (Prince 1983).

THE DEFINITION OF AN ETHNIC DISORDER

In recent years the term 'ethnicity' has increasingly been in use in an attempt to overcome some of the difficulties that surround the definition of culture. However, the term proved to be an equally problematic one.

Ethnicity, which is often confused with race or nationality, refers to a socially constructed phenomenon that implies shared and distinctive traditions that are maintained between generations and lead to a sense of a group identity.

Devereux introduced the term ethnic disorder in 1955, suggesting a terminology that is perhaps more sociologically meaningful than is culture-bound syndrome. For him an ethnic disorder has its own dynamics that represent core contradictions and anxieties in a particular society. The symptoms of the disorder are exaggerations of normal attitudes and behaviours that are prevalent in the culture. There are clear common grounds between Devereux's ethnic disorder and the meaning-centred approach to culture-bound syndromes.

However, before making any attempt to apply any of the above models to eating disorders, I need to address two important aspects which are highly relevant to this argument:

1 the changes in the definition of normal and abnormal over the course of time;
2 the change or the metamorphosis of pathology secondary to changes in social conditions.

THE PATHOLOGIZATION OF EATING BEHAVIOURS OVER TIME

The meaning-centred approach to culture boundedness focused on the relativity of normal and abnormal across cultures; however, this relativity is perhaps more temporal than cultural. It has been suggested that, with the passage of time, phenomenona that are considered culturally acceptable become increasingly more abnormal and assume morbid proportions. In one of my articles entitled 'Prescription of vomiting', I explained how vomiting and the use of purgatives were historically widely prevalent behaviours (Nasser 1993). They were largely accepted and even prescribed by physicians, in keeping with the prevailing cultural values at the time. The first prescriptions of vomiting can be traced back to the Egyptian Ebers papyrus which was dedicated to the virtues of emesis since 'all diseases to which men were subject proceed from food itself' (Garrison 1929).

In the *Syriac Book of Medicine*, vomiting was advocated for the healing of the bestial lust for food. The episodic ingestion of considerable amounts of food was referred to as Bulimos (Budge and Wallis 1913). Hippocrates advised the use of vomiting for two consecutive days each month. In his book on human nature he says 'The doctor must know which are the ailments, if they are due to fullness, they are cured by evacuation' (cited in Berthe 1909). As for the Romans, they are famously known for their invention of the vomitorium which allowed them to indulge in excessive eating and relieve themselves by vomiting. This emphasis on the therapeutic value of vomiting carried on in Arabic medicine. In the *Canon of Medicine*, Avicenna recommended inducing vomiting if one ate to excess: 'When a state of over-repletion exists then there will be a need for rapid emesis; the use of finger or feather will incite the movement or tickling the throat gently'. He interestingly thought that self-induced vomiting was a good method for treating the flabbiness of the body. He warned nonetheless against developing the habit of doing it regularly and frequently: 'The custom of some people who eat to excess and then procure vomiting is one of the things that ends in a chronic disorder' (cited in Gruner 1930).

Purgation went hand in hand with vomiting, and the use of cathartic drugs dominated the therapeutic scene in Europe. This was satirized by Molière who wrapped it up in the Latin formula (*clysterium donare, postea saignare, ensuita purgare*) which vaguely translates to 'give enema, then bleed and finally purge' (Berthe 1909).

It is clear that the perception of the use of vomiting and purgation changed over time from being healthy or even advisable to a morbid phenomenon.

History is also full of cases of self-starvation for religious reasons. The most famous reports of religious fasting are those of self-starvation in mediaeval Italy. Religious self-starvation is a form of self-denial, a quest to harness the body and achieve triumph for the soul. Lacey (1982) drew on the legend of St Wilgfortis, who starved herself until she grew a beard and developed a hairy body. When her father in his uncontrolled rage had her crucified, she claimed to have been liberated from the 'passion that encumbrance all women'; historians claim that menstruation was what she meant. Rampling (1985) also referred to the fourteenth century St Catherine of Sienna, whose asceticism was the height of perfection. This struggle for perfection was symbolized in her eating behaviour: 'It was a greater suffering for her to take food, than for a starving man to be deprived of it' (cited in Raymond 1980).

A study carried out by Bell (1985) on several hundred Italian female saints of the Catholic church suggests that fasting behaviour is closely related to social perception. These cases of historical self-starvation were accepted in the past as mere religious experiences. There is a tendency nowadays to view them as early accounts of cases of anorexia nervosa, and they are now referred to as 'holy anorexia'.

I describe these historical accounts of vomiting, purging and self-starvation to demonstrate how certain behaviours evolve in the course of time to assume the status of illness.

THE CASE OF HYSTERIA

The changes in the perception and the definition of the morbid over time seem to imply sociocultural changes as well as to reflect changes in social preoccupations. This is clearly seen in the relationship between anorexia nervosa and hysteria. It is interesting that at the time of describing the syndrome of anorexia nervosa, it was thought to be a manifestation of hysteria. Gull (1874) initially gave it the name *apepsia hysterica*. Lasegue (1873) called it *anorexie hystérique*, and Gilles de la Tourette (1895) viewed it as 'digestive trouble frequent in hysterics'.

The apparent rise in the occurrence of the syndrome of anorexia nervosa has been mirrored by a decline in the incidence of hysteria. It has been argued that both hysteria and anorexia nervosa represent forms of life adaptation which make a psychological statement. Hysteria was commonly thought to be the product of a sexually repressive society and was prevalent and is still to be found in societies where the atmosphere is generally regarded as sexually repressive. The anorexic position on the other hand, could be seen as the product of contemporary society's expectations and demands for thinness (Swartz *et al.* 1983).

Similarly, Loudon (1980) thought that the old condition of chlorosis, which used to affect vulnerable young girls in earlier times, manifesting with anaemia and yellowish discoloration, has also been replaced by anorexia nervosa. Interestingly, some of the doubts expressed about the similarity between chlorosis and anorexia nervosa are based on the simple fact that chlorosis was a condition known to affect girls from low socio-economic classes – in contrast to anorexia nervosa, which is associated with more upper socio-economic classes.

Russell was more inclined to the view that there is a connection between anorexia nervosa and hysteria or indeed neurosis in general. They all appear to be different expressions of neurotic distress that is shaped by the prevailing culture. The need to address this issue became greater after anorexia nervosa had itself undergone changes in presentation with the evolution of the bulimic syndrome:

> We must therefore return to the likelihood that neurotic illness is more often expressed nowadays as anorexia nervosa or a bulimic disorder. We should also explore the mechanisms underlying these transformations and consider the operation of pathoplastic causal factors.
>
> (Russell 1985)

Cultural forces were therefore considered capable of moulding the presentation of the neurotic disorder, as if neurotic disorders follow changing fashion (Hare 1981) or have a contemporary style (Jaspers 1959). These forces are not pathogenic but pathoplastic, i.e. influencing the content, the colouring and the form of the illness.

The desirability of thinness and the changes in the position of women in modern society can exercise this pathoplastic role on neurotic illness to produce eating psychopathology. The pathogenic force, however, i.e. the necessary cause for these disorders, remains elusive.

Some disagree with the whole notion that anorexia nervosa is a psychiatric disorder even if the contribution of culture to its pathoplasticity is taken into account. Their objection is based on the fact that the process of medicalization is only helping to reinforce the underlying oppressive social patterns that have been responsible in causing it in the first place (Orbach 1986). It has been argued that self-starvation should be seen in the context of the social and cultural meaning that non-eating has for women (Robertson 1992). Anorexia nervosa is therefore regarded as a socially adaptive condition on which a variety of professionals should have an equal claim to understand and treat it.

It is interesting that women were considered particula:ly vulnerable to the development of culture-bound psychopathology:

It is perhaps not surprising that culture-bound syndromes are found in women in male orientated societies . . . a culturally excluded group prevented from participating in the dominant culture through which everyday individual identity is attained. Thus perforce they have resorted to mystical sanctions outside everyday jural relationships and power.

(Littlewood 1986)

EATING DISORDERS – CULTURE BOUND, ETHNIC DISORDER OR REACTIVE TO CULTURE CHANGE?

Prince (1983) argued that an eating disorder as described in western literature has all the criteria that makes it a culture-bound syndrome:

As westerners we all experience first hand the powerful anorexic influences that are currently playing upon us, particularly upon the western female. The slim youthful body is beautiful and healthy. The fat person is slovenly, ugly, prone to disease and lacks self discipline.

He argued that there is reluctance from orthodox western psychiatry to regard eating disorders as culture bound, because of the ethnocentric bias that only true psychiatric syndromes occur in the West: 'Culture-bound syndromes are what other people have, not us' (Hahn 1983).

In keeping with the views of the traditional school, Prince based his argument mainly on the apparent epidemiologic evidence:

namely, the restriction of the presence of the disorder to certain cultural groups and its presumed absence in others. The epidemiologic evidence for the culture-boundedness of eating disorders is not sufficient, as it could easily be challenged if these disorders were to turn out to be happening elsewhere – which we will find out in the next chapter. However, the meaning-centred approach to the definition would still carry some weight. Prince acknowledged the significance of the cultural meaning of eating disorders but questioned the pathogenic force within culture.

To problematize the argument even further, Prince should have also considered that cultures, too, are constantly changing. This is important in the discussion of non-western cultures; there is a tendency to view these cultures as fixed and static and possibly not to have changed or moved-on since the accounts made by nineteenth century European travellers or those of anthropologists that were limited to truly particular groups where the findings cannot in any way be generalized to the rest of the relevant population.

However, despite all limitations, the issue as Swartz (1985) put it is not whether eating disorders are culture bound or not; the debate is more to do with how useful this concept is in providing us with a framework for understanding these disorders from a social perspective. While it is true that disordered eating revolves around the notion of thinness which is cherished and glorified by the prevailing culture, the disorders express themselves in varying degrees of severity. They blur and merge with normative, culturally acceptable modes of behaviour like dieting. It is also clear that these disorders are gender specific, which may have something to do with women's position and perception of their role and value within society (Nasser 1988, Gordon 1990).

If we go back again to Devereux's model of ethnic disorder, we can find that there are elements within this model that clearly apply to eating disorders. Gordon (1990), in his book *Anorexia and Bulimia – Anatomy of a Social Epidemic*, demonstrates his enthusiasm for the concept of an ethnic disorder and advocates it as an appropriate model for understanding eating pathology. He suggests a diagnostic framework based on the following key elements.

1 The disorder occurs frequently in the culture in question, particularly relative to other psychiatric disorders.

2 The disorder expresses core conflicts and psychological tensions that are pervasive in the culture.

3 The disorder is a final common pathway for expression of a wide variety of idiosyncratic personal problems.

4 The disorder is a highly patterned and widely imitated model for the expression of distress.

5 The symptoms of the disorder are exaggerations of normal attitudes and behaviours within the culture and promoted by the prevailing climate of opinion, primarily the media.

The argument for the ethnic nature of eating disorders is a plausible one, and yet it is like the meaning-centred approach to culture boundedness in being fundamentally based on the absence of these disorders in other cultures. Nearly all thinkers in the field of culture and eating pathology used this apparent absence of eating disorders in other cultures as a sufficient criterion for the culture specificity of such disorders. Obviously, this is now being challenged on the basis of the new epidemiologic evidence that points to the emergence of these syndromes in the so-called non-western societies. Identification with the western cultural norms in this respect was one of the early explanations for the emergence of eating pathology in cultures that were considered initially protected from developing them (Nasser 1988).

Orphan cases – i.e. cases which occur among people who are geographically and culturally distant from the area in which any culture-bound version of the syndrome is endemic – are likely to be important for the development of a model of the syndrome. These orphan cases in the context of eating disorders would be expected to occur in developing countries or among immigrants from these countries to more developed ones (Taylor 1985). It has been argued that these orphan cases develop in reaction to culture change. The culture change here is secondary to evolution or human migration (Di Nicola 1990).

Although the term 'acculturation' commonly refers to the identification of a small group with the values of the larger group, this acculturation process does not necessarily take place only through migration. It has indeed been going on in non-western societies for a long time, precisely since colonial times. It is also taking place now through identification with universal values disseminated through the media, and cultures are subsequently becoming increasingly similar.

This is not an attempt to undermine the particularities within any individual culture or indeed to subscribe to the traditional transcultural school of thought that dismisses any phenomenon that does not comply with its rules. However, the meaning-centred approach to culture and psychopathology has been more inclined to emphasize differences, possibly at the expense of understanding what was truly happening in other societies. In my opinion this has led to lack of attention to similarities between societies, with subsequent limited insight into the role of society in shaping human distress. In many instances social disadvantage related to class, education, or unemployment have been taken to represent general cultural traits. There is therefore an urgent need to refine our approaches to the definition of culture. There are mechanisms that are now in operation continually defining and redefining culture.

The adoption by the majority of societies of one economic system, and the contribution of the deregulated media to standardizing our value systems, are the two current major forces. These issues will be discussed in some depth later on. What is clear perhaps now is that the argument for the culture boundedness of eating disorders is no longer convincing. However, it is true to say that culture change has contributed to the shaping of neurosis which led to the emergence of eating disorders. This culture change is no longer unique to one particular culture or society; it has indeed become global.

Chapter 3

The emergence of eating disorders in other cultures/societies

One of the major aspects of the culture specificity of eating disorders, as discussed in the previous chapter, is their assumed rarity in non-western societies. Non-western cultures have long been considered relatively immune from developing eating disorders, by reasons of different authentic cultural values that do not overvalue thinness and possibly associate plumpness with positive attributes of wealth, fertility and femininity. Even obesity in some societies was once seen to reflect desirable sexual characteristics (Ford and Beach 1952, Rudofsky 1972).

The majority of non-western societies also have developing economies; hence they are considered protected from disorders commonly associated with affluence. More important, however, is the view that gender roles in these societies are thought to be clearly defined, and therefore their women should not in theory have the conflicts over gender definition that is seen by the feminist theorists to be at the heart of the vulnerability of modern western women to eating pathology.

These were the long-held beliefs that formed the basis of the view that eating disorders were rare in non-western cultures. Some studies published from non-western countries in the 1960s and early 1970s provided support for this view (El-Sarrag 1968, Okasha et al. 1977). However, these studies were subject to the methodological flaw that they clearly lacked a definition of the syndrome of anorexia nervosa, which was often regarded as a form of hysteria and not a specific psychiatric entity.

Other sources of information on this subject were initially limited to case reports of individuals from different ethnic backgrounds living in the UK or North America. There was a clear need for further investigation based on scientific principles to test whether this rarity was genuine or not. This led to several attempts to assess the incidence, prevalence and comparative prevalence of these disorders in different societies. One of the objectives of these studies was to find out whether there has been any recent change in culture and the impact of this change on women's perception of their bodies and indeed their weight preferences.

REPORTS OF EATING DISORDERS AMONG ETHNIC GROUPS IN BRITAIN, NORTH AMERICA AND ELSEWHERE

Bruch (1966) was the first to draw attention to the conspicuous absence of Negro patients among her anorexic population. This observation raised interest in the subject, and subsequently several reports were made of black girls diagnosed as having anorexia nervosa in the USA (Jones et al. 1980, Pumariega et al. 1984, Robinson and Andersen 1985, Andersen and Hay 1985, Hsu 1987).

Similar reports were also published in the UK (Thomas and Szmukler 1985, Holden and Robinson 1988, Lacey and Dolan 1988). The authors of these reports commented on certain aspects of these cases which could be relevant to their eating pathology: namely the higher incidence of parental separation and the presence of other family problems in those patients' backgrounds. The family disturbance was apparently related to racial identity. Some cases were described as having been fostered for a long period by white mothers, speculating that their exposure to their white mothers' values in relation to weight may have sensitized them towards developing this psychopathology (Lacey and Dolan 1988).

There was also a tendency for those black patients to show more bulimic features and to be older than the white anorexics at the onset of the disorder. More interesting was the description of the black anorexics as achievement oriented, aspiring to higher social status than their parents. The girls also saw themselves as somewhat responsible for 'correcting the image of the blacks' in general. They had a powerful need to fit into society and thought that this integration was only possible through rigid dieting and the adoption of the prevailing social standards of thinness (Silber 1986).

The reports of black anorexic patients in the USA initially overshadowed the need to assess the existence of this problem among other racial groups, particularly native Americans and Hispanic minorities. In subsequent reports, cases of anorexia nervosa were found among native Americans (Yates 1989, Silber 1986). The authors were surprised by the severity of their patients' thinness and commented that it seemed to be 'a repudiation of the image of the traditional woman on the reservation'.

The desire to fit into a society where thinness is considered a vehicle to acceptance and success was offered as an explanation of the finding of two cases of eating disorders among Jewish immigrant women from Soviet origins, who developed the disorder within two years of their immigration from the old Soviet Union to the USA (Bulik 1987). The impact of immigration on the development of eating pathology was further highlighted in another report of three Vietnamese refugees who also developed their eating disorder within a short time of their arrival in the USA (Kope and Sack 1987).

These reports clearly showed that eating disorders did occur among ethnic minorities living in the UK and the USA. The frequency of presentation, however, judged by the number of these reports, was still much less than would be expected in the white community. It is well known that case reports underestimate the true magnitude of any medical problem in the community (Goldberg and Huxley 1980). One of the reasons is that not everyone with a problem will ask for medical help. It has also been suspected that those who have eating disorders from ethnic minorities could be reluctant to seek help from specialist white services. Also, these disorders may not be easily identified by primary care physicians, because they assume that they are rare in these ethnic groups.

The cases reported among minority groups in Britain and the USA were not mirrored by reports of cases of eating disorders developing in their own native countries. It is difficult to know whether this state of under-reporting reflected a genuine absence of these disorders. Under-reporting in general could be caused by the lack of awareness of the existence of a problem, which could easily lead to misdiagnosis. However the situation is continually changing, and cases of eating disorders have increasingly been reported. Whether this is to do with increased awareness, or indeed the emergence of a problem that did not exist before, is difficult to tell.

Some interesting cases have since been reported from Nigeria, Zimbabwe, Hong Kong, Malaysia and the United Arab Emirates

(Nwaefuna1981, Buchan and Gregory 1984, Famuyiwa 1988, Lee *et al.* 1992, Schmidt 1993, Abou-Saleh *et al.* in press). Exposure to western society, high achievement orientation and a possible history of pre-morbid obesity are significant elements that seem to be common to all the cases reported.

BODY IMAGE AND ETHNICITY

The majority of case reports implied that vulnerability to the development of eating disorders may have increased among individuals from non-western backgrounds by virtue of living in the West. Even the cases reported from non-western countries also pointed to the exposure of the affected girls to western societies while receiving part of their education in the West or through their parents' employment there.

The relationship between culture change and weight consciousness was first studied in the late 1960s, where an inverse relationship was found between obesity and the length of exposure to American society. Susceptibility to culture changes was not found to be the same for all ethnicities. Obesity, for instance, was more prevalent in American females of Italian descent than those of British origin, and similar findings were reported when those of Czech origin were compared with those of Polish origin. One of the explanations for the difference between the Czechs and the Poles was that the latter were thought to be more easily Americanized (Goldblatt *et al.* 1965).

Contrary to earlier assumptions, girls of east European origin living in Australia were also found to view obesity negatively, as did their Anglo-Celtic counterparts. Attention was drawn in this study to the fact that girls tended to show more readiness than boys to adapt to the new weight values of Australian society (Worsley 1981).

In a more recent study, American black and white women were investigated for their body shape preferences. The initial hypothesis was that African American women would be different from white American women in this respect. The results showed, however, both groups to share similar body type preferences and to have equally high levels of body dissatisfaction (Strauss *et al.* 1994). This was also the case when white Americans were compared for their body shape preferences with Costa Rican and Japanese

Table 3.1 Case reports of eating disorders in ethnic groups

Country	Author	Number of cases	AN/BN[a]	Ethnicity	Characteristics
USA	Jones et al. (1980)	1	AN	Black	—
	Pumariega et al. (1984)	2	AN	Black	Family pathology
	Robinson and Andersen (1985)	5[c]	1 AN 4 BN	Black	Family pathology
	Andersen and Hay (1985)	8	1 AN 7 BN	Black	Late onset
	Hsu (1987)	7[b]	4 AN 3 BN	Black	Middle class backgrounds
	Silber (1986)	7	AN	5 Hispanics 2 Blacks	Achievement orientation
	Bulik (1986)	2	1 AN 1 BN	Jewish Soviet immigrants	Impact of immigration
	Kope and Sack (1981)	3	AN	Vietnamese refugees	Impact of immigration

UK	Thomas and Szmukler (1983)	3	Black	2 AN 1 BN	Achievement orientation
	Holden and Robinson (1988)	13	8 Indians, 1 African, 4 mixed race	11 BN 2 AN	Achievement orientation
	Lacey and Dolan (1988)	5	Different ethnic backgrounds	BN	Difficulties with racial identity
Other countries	Nwaefuna (1981)	1	Black Nigerian	AN	Onset at pregnancy
	Famuyiwa (1988)	2	Black Nigerian	AN	Psychosexual conflicts
	Buchan and Gregory (1984)	1	Zimbabwean black	AN	Achievement orientation
	Schmidt (1993)	3[b]	2 Hong Kong 1 Malaysian	BN	Premorbid obesity
	Lee et al. (1989)	3	3 Hong Kong	AN	Westernization
	Lee et al. (1992)	4	4 Hong Kong	BN	Westernization
	Abou Saleh (in press)	5[c]	Mixed Arab	AN	Impact of cultural change

[a] AN = anorexia nervosa, BN = bulimia nervosa
[b] One case of male anorexic
[c] Two cases of male anorexics

students living in the USA. No differences in body image were observed between the three cultural groups (Gustavson *et al.* 1993).

In Britain, Kenyan Asians and Kenyan British were compared for their desired body image. The British Kenyans evaluated larger figures negatively compared with Kenyan Asians (Furnham and Alibhai 1983). The inference made from this study was that exposure to British values in connection to weight induced a change in the British Kenyan's perception of what is consiaered a desirable body weight. In keeping with this observation, Asian women in Britain were found to be similar to Caucasians in their concern over their body shape (Dolan *et al.* 1990). Also, Nigerian women in Britain desired body weight which was less than their matched counterparts in Nigeria (Toriola *et al.* unpublished).

These studies clearly imply that the western ideal of female body shape has permeated other ethnic groups, a process possibly facilitated by successive acculturation. However, the impact of the assimilation of western cultural norms in relation to weight was commonly investigated in ethnic groups living in a western society, except for one study that was carried out on Egyptian students attending the American University in Cairo. The students were appraised for their body shape preference on the assumption that the American University environment would make them more exposed to somewhat less traditional values. The female students felt that their ideal shape should significantly be thinner than their current shape, while male students did not. The authors concluded that the body shape preference encountered in this population was not different from that of the American population (Ford *et al.* 1990).

Case reports of eating disorders in ethnic groups are summarized in Table 3.1.

THE PREVALENCE OF EATING DISORDERS IN NON-WESTERN SOCIETIES

The Middle East

Egypt

The relationship between exposure to western cultural norms in connection to weight and vulnerability to eating disorders was first put to test when two matched groups of Arab female students attending London and Cairo Universities were compared for their eating attitudes. The method of investigation was similar to that of other studies carried out on student populations at that time. Morbid concern over weight as measured by a positive score on the Eating Attitude Test questionnaire (EAT) was found in 12 per cent of the Cairo group and 22 per cent of the London-Arab group. These figures were higher than reported in contemporary UK student studies. Six cases of bulimia nervosa were identified in the London-Arab group but none in Cairo. The study showed that concern with body weight was in existence in a society presumed to have different values in this respect. Identification with western cultural norms in relation to body weight was thought to be partly responsible for causing this concern, which resulted in the emergence of actual clinical cases in the group that was more exposed to these norms (Nasser 1986, 1988).

In view of the unexpectedly high percentage of EAT positive scorers in the above-mentioned study, there was a need to substantiate the results by repeating the study on a larger sample. A sample of 15-year-old Egyptian secondary school girls was screened for abnormal eating attitudes, again using an Arabic translation of the EAT questionnaire. The choice of this particular age group was to enable direct comparison with studies conducted on similar age groups in the UK (Mann *et al.* 1983, Szmukler 1983, Johnson-Sabine *et al.* 1988). The percentage of those who had a positive score on the EAT (11.4 per cent) was closely similar to that for the Cairo group in the earlier study and was higher than those reported in studies conducted on white British populations. All the girls who had a positive score on the EAT admitted to repeated dieting and had clear knowledge of various diets and slimming pills on the market. Their reason for dieting was a desire to be slimmer and more attractive. A total of 3.4 per cent of them showed enough concern about their weight, dieted, used laxatives or slimming pills to make them qualify for a diagnosis of an atypical eating disorder or partial syndrome. Only 1.2 per cent of the sample showed sufficient clinical features to fulfil the diagnosis of bulimia nervosa (Nasser 1994a).

Israel

Arab school girls were also among those investigated in a later study conducted in Israel. The objective of the study was to examine the eating attitudes of Arab and Jewish Israeli schoolgirls.

The EAT was also used after translation into Arabic and Hebrew and the results were rather interesting. It was found that the degree of resemblance between the schoolgirls' eating behaviour and the morbid behaviour of the diagnosed eating disorders cases depended on the degree of exposure to western body ideals and the presence of conflict between what is modern and traditional in relation to the female role. Interestingly the kibbutz population, followed by all the Arabs (except Circasians), showed abnormalities in eating attitudes. The female kibbutzim had the highest EAT scores (27.3 per cent) followed by the Arab Muslims (18.6 per cent). The findings were explained on the basis that the Arabs showed strong western influences in their attitudes, particularly to body image, which could make them easily prone to developing eating disorders. They nonetheless concluded that the group that was most at risk was the kibbutz group (Apter et al. 1994).

It is interesting that in the early years of the kibbutz, until 1965, anorexia nervosa was considered rare. However, over a 25-year period the annual incidence of anorexia nervosa increased by eight hundred per cent. The authors speculated that the increase in the incidence of eating pathology among the female kibbutzim was related to changes in the structure of the kibbutz itself with reference to an increase in food consumption and also changes in women's perception of their role (Kaffman and Sadeh 1989).

Greece and Turkey

The eating attitudes of Greek students in the Greek towns of Veria and Ioannina were compared with those of Greek students living in Munich. In this study the Anorexia Nervosa Inventory for Self Rating (ANIS) was used. Those who had a significant score on the questionnaire and showed evidence of weight loss were clinically interviewed. Surprisingly, the female population of two Greek samples in Greece had significantly higher questionnaire scores than the female Greek sample in Munich, indicating that the Greeks in Greece showed more figure consciousness and dieting behaviour than those in Munich. However, there were more cases of anorexia nervosa identified among the Greeks in Munich than Greek girls in Greece. The lower questionnaire scores in the Munich sample were therefore explained on the basis that the

Greek girls there were probably more clever in hiding their abnormal eating tendencies. The findings were attributed to greater exposure to western ideals, which increased the risk of developing eating disorders (Fichter *et al.* 1983).

The same hypothesis was tested when the investigators compared the above three populations with a Turkish student population in Istanbul. The Turkish group showed lower scores on the questionnaire, which was attributed to lower exposure of the Turkish adolescents in Istanbul to the western ideals of slimness than was the case for Greeks in Greece and Greeks in Germany (Fichter *et al.* 1988).

The Far East

Japan

Several surveys of abnormal eating attitudes among Japanese students were carried out (Nogami *et al.* 1984, Kamata *et al.* 1987, Nakane and Umino 1987). They all suggested that concern with weight and disordered eating patterns are emerging in Japanese society, and the prevalence of this disturbance could be even higher in Japan than in the West. A significantly high percentage of positive EAT scorers (35 per cent) was reported in one study (Mukai *et al.* 1994). Further, these disorders were shown to be on the increase: a one hundred per cent increase in the incidence of anorexia nervosa over a five year period was reported in one study (Suematsue *et al.* 1985). The level of urbanization was demonstrated to affect the incidence of anorexia nervosa: it was clearly higher in cities than in rural areas of Japan (Azuma and Henmi 1982, Ohzeki *et al.* 1990).

The pattern of eating disorder reported in the majority of these studies is consistent with bulimia. In one study, binge eating was found in 7.8 per cent of the sample, and 1.4 per cent used vomiting as a means of keeping their weight under control (Nogami *et al.* 1984). These findings were rather surprising as they were thought to be incompatible with Japanese cultural values.

Indian subcontinent

Indians, Pakistanis and Bangladeshis (commonly referred to in research as 'Asian') constitute the largest immigrant population in the UK and were understandably an interesting group to study in connection with eating disorders. Asian and white schoolgirls in Bradford were surveyed for abnormalities in eating attitudes, using the EAT questionnaire. The Asian girls' families were mostly from Pakistan; however, the majority of the girls were born in the UK and all received their secondary school education there. This study showed rather surprisingly that the EAT scores of the Asian girls were higher than those of the Caucasian group (15 per cent and 12 per cent respectively). Only one Asian girl was diagnosed as having anorexia nervosa, whereas seven Asian and two white girls received a diagnosis of bulimia nervosa (Mumford and Whitehouse 1988).

Asian girls from more traditional backgrounds were found to be more at risk of developing an eating disorder than those who come from more westernized families, contrary to previous suggestions. However, in another study conducted in Lahore, Pakistan, the girls who were most westernized appeared to be more at risk of developing an eating disorder (Mumford et al. 1991).

More cases of bulimic behaviour were also found among Asian schoolgirls than Caucasians in further studies conducted on mixed populations of schoolgirls (Ahmad et al. 1994, McCourt and Waller 1995). However, possible cultural differences in eating attitudes between the Asians and Caucasians were suspected in a comparable study carried out in Canada, where the Caucasians were found to be 5.5 per cent more likely to score positively on the EAT than the Asians (Lucero et al. 1992).

China

In a survey conducted by the psychiatric epidemiology unit at the Chinese University of Hong Kong, only one case of anorexia nervosa was found. This was in keeping with the overall impression that eating disorders are still considered rare in China. The rarity was explained on the basis that the majority of Chinese girls are slim anyway, if not underweight by western standards. A comparison of the ideal weight charts showed more than 5 per cent difference between Chinese and western girls of the same height (Lee et al. 1989).

However, some cases of eating disorders were still found among the Chinese population. The Chinese constituted two thirds of the identified anorexic cases in Malaysia, which was attributed to their higher level of urbanization and affluence in relation to other ethnicities there (Buhrich 1981).

Cases of anorexia and bulimia nervosa were also reported among Chinese women in Singapore and Hong Kong. Some of the cases, however, did not have body image distortion and were thought to be milder in their presentation compared with the western anorexics (Ong *et al.* 1982, Lee *et al.* 1989, Schmidt 1993).

Africa

A number of eating disorders studies were conducted on blacks living in the USA. The question of how representative this group is of its African origin is a major issue in all these studies and has important implications for the results.

Some surveys only focused on the prevalence of dieting, vomiting or purging in both black and white populations. In some studies, dieting behaviour was equal among black and white females (Gray *et al.* 1987). This was not the case in a study carried out in Zimbabwe, where anorexic and anorexic-like behaviours were found to be more common in white or mixed race students than in black ones (Hooper and Garner 1986).

Bulimic behaviours, on the other hand, were significantly found to be more prevalent in black than in white girls, except for one study which showed cases of bulimia in the white population to outnumber those of the black women (Gray *et al.* 1987). The tendency for the black women to develop more bulimia is clearly reflected in the majority of the cases reported in the black communities in both Britain and the USA (Robinson and Andersen 1985, Lacey and Dolan 1988).

This was confirmed in a recent study conducted in Britain where dysfunctional eating patterns, with a tendency to develop bulimia, were found to be more prevalent in the African-Caribbean population than the white British (Reiss 1996). High rates of bulimic behaviour were also found among high school and university student populations in Nigeria (Oyewumi and Kazarian, 1992).

The bulimic behaviour tended, however, to be different for white and black girls. While there was a tendency for the white girls to use vomiting, black girls tended to use laxatives instead. Racial differences were suggested to play a role in determining the nature of the bulimic behaviour (Emmons 1992).

In general, eating pathology in the black community was found to reflect an actual weight problem for the black females and was more related to the degree to which the black women assimilated the white mainstream culture (Abrams *et al.* 1993).

South America

There is growing interest in studying eating disorders in South America, because of increased recognition that it is becoming a major health problem. Cases of anorexia nervosa were found among the upper socio-economic classes in Chile and Brazil (Pumarino and Vivanco 1982, Nunes *et al.* 1991). However, these studies are still very few and mostly unpublished. Argentina in particular seems to be facing a rise in the incidence of these disorders, which has led to the appearance of specialized eating disorders units such as the Association Against Bulimia and Anorexia (ALUBA). This is partly blamed on the influence of the media where so much emphasis is placed on women's thinness as equivalent to attractiveness. The majority of the Argentinian girls are described as fashion and figure conscious. In a recent study carried out on a secondary school population in Buenos Aires, 29 per cent of the female student population had a positive score on the Eating Attitude Test questionnaire (EAT) and thought to have a diagnosis of an atypical eating disorder. Nine per cent of those high scorers were found to fulfil the criteria for a full eating disorder syndrome (Bello unpublished).

However, most of the published studies were on Hispanics living in the USA. The question of how representative the American Hispanics are of their origin is as contentious as it is for the blacks in the USA. The authors of a study published under the title 'Minorities join the majorities' recognized the rapidly growing problem of eating disorders among minority groups in the USA. In this study, binge eating behaviour was found to be highest in native Americans (14 per cent), followed by the Hispanics (13 per cent) and the whites (10 per cent) (Smith and Krejci 1991).

The relationship between the Hispanics' vulnerability to eating disorders and the adoption of American values was investigated in an earlier study. In the Hispanic group a correlation was found between the level of acculturation and morbid concern over weight as measured by EAT scores (Pumariega *et al.* 1986). Again

Table 3.2 Eating disorders in non-western countries

Study	Sample	Score	Estimated prevalence
Mukai *et al.* (1994)	Japanese schoolgirls	35% EAT + ve	—
King and Bhugra (1989)	School and college students in India	29% EAT + ve	—
Mumford *et al.* (1992)	Schoolgirls in Lahore[a]	—	1.6%
Bello (unpublished)	Schoolgirls in Buenos Aires	29% EAT + ve	9%
Nasser (1994a)	Schoolgirls in Cairo	11.4% EAT + ve	1.2% full syndrome 3.4% subclinical
Apter *et al.* (1994)	High school Arab and Jewish girls	27.3% kibbutz EAT + ve 18.6% Arab Moslem EAT + ve	—
Oyewumi and Kazarian (1992)	High school, university undergraduates in Nigeria	21.2% bingers[b] 22.2% vomiters	—

[a] EAT administered in English
[b] The instrument used here was The Binge Eating Questionnaire

this study suggested that greater adherence to western culture could increase individuals' vulnerability to eating disorders.

Studies of eating disorders in non-western countries are summarized in Table 3.2. Comparative prevalence findings for groups related by ethnicity or country of residence are shown in Table 3.3.

PREVALENCE OF EATING DISORDERS IN EUROPE

The bulk of the early epidemiological work from the western hemisphere emerged mainly from Britain, the USA and Canada, except for two major studies from Sweden and Switzerland that significantly showed that the incidence of anorexia nervosa was steadily on the increase (Theander 1970, Willi and Grossman 1983).

Table 3.3 Eating disorders – comparative prevalence

Author	Study	Method	Findings
Fichter et al. (1983)	Greek in Munich/Greek in Greece	ANIS[a] and clinical interviews	>cases of AN among Greeks in Munich (1.1%, 0.4% and 0.35%)
Nasser (1986)	Arabs in Egypt/Arabs in London	EAT and clinical interviews	6 cases of BN in Arab-London group. None in Cairo
Pumariega (1986)	Hispanic/white in USA	EAT	Comparable eating attitude/eating pathology ∝ level of acculturation
Gray et al. (1987)	Black/white in USA	Designed questionnaire	>cases of BN among white (13% and 3%)
Mumford and Whitehouse (1988)	Asian/Caucasian in Britain	EAT and clinical interviews	>cases of BN among Asians (3.4% and 0.6%)
Smith and Krejci (1990)	Hispanic/Native American and White in USA	EDI[b]	Native > Hispanic > White American (14% > 13% > 10%)
Lucero et al. (1992)	Asian/Caucasian in Canada	EAT and clinical interviews	>dysfunctional eating in Caucasians
Emmons (1992)	Black/white in USA (dieting and purging)	Designed questionnaire	W > B – vomiting B > W – purging
Abrams et al. (1993)	Black/white in USA	EDI	>Abnormal attitudes in white. Eating pathology in blacks ∝ degrees of assimilation of white culture
Reiss (1996)	African-Caribbean/white population in Britain	BITE[c]	>Dysfunctional eating in African-Caribbean

[a] ANIS   Anorexia Nervosa Inventory for self-rating, validated for use in German populations
[b] EDI   A 64 item self-report measure. Similar to the EAT but assesses other psychological behavioural disturbances
[c] BITE   A self-report measure for bulimia
W = White, B = Black, BN = bulimia nervosa, AN = anorexia nervosa

In Britain, the incidence of anorexia nervosa was calculated from case register and hospital records data and was shown to be in the range 2–4 per 100,000 (Szmukler *et al.* 1984, Williams and King 1987). The majority of the epidemiological research, however, was carried out in the community in an attempt to obtain more reliable information about the true magnitude of this problem in society. From these studies the prevalence figure for anorexia nervosa was 1 per cent and bulimia nervosa 1–1.9 per cent (Cooper and Fairburn 1983, King 1986). In the absence of the full eating disorders syndromes, studies were also able to show that concerns with food and body weight were relatively common in student and general practice populations and the prevalence rate for the subclinical syndrome was estimated to be in the region of 2–5 per cent (Button and Whitehouse 1981, Mann *et al.* 1983, Szmukler 1983, Clarke and Palmer 1983, Johnson-Sabine *et al.* 1988, King 1989).

In recent years, several studies emerged from European countries other than Britain which showed a general increase in the incidence of eating disorders, particularly bulimia nervosa (Cullberg and Engström-Lindberg 1988, Willi *et al.* 1990). Attention was rightly drawn to the fact that early European research could have easily underestimated the true rates of these disorders in society, as it was mainly based on case register data. This is especially so in the case of bulimia nervosa as only a small proportion of patients are admitted to hospital compared with those with anorexia nervosa (Joergensen 1992).

The increase in the incidence of bulimia nervosa in the Netherlands was found to be higher in larger cities, giving rise to speculation that the level of urbanization could be a possible risk factor for bulimia nervosa (Hoek *et al.* 1995).

Also, the prevalence of eating disturbance, particularly those for the subclinical syndrome, was found to be relatively high in the city of Rome (Cuzzolaro 1991). However, the prevalence pattern of eating disorders in the Austrian Tyrol and rural Italy was broadly similar to that reported in metropolitan areas, highlighting the need for more epidemiological studies to further explore this urban/rural issue (Rathner and Messner 1993).

In European community studies, bulimic behaviours were consistently shown to be fairly common. In Denmark, for instance, binge eating and pathological weight reducing measures were found to be relatively common among medical students who incidentally did not regard their low weight as particularly abnormal (Waadegaard and Petersson 1995). Also, bulimic behaviours were found to be common in France and tended to occur more in older women (Tordjman *et al.* 1994), although the incidence of bulimia in France was still seen to be much lower than its incidence in the United States. This was explained on the basis of possible cultural differences between the two countries in relation to the meaning and value of food and its consumption (Ledoux *et al.* 1991).

US studies have always shown higher level of eating disorders than in Britain and the rest of Europe. The rates vary from 8.2 per 100,000 in North America to 0.08 per 100,000 in Sweden (Theander 1970, Lucas *et al.* 1988). This made European research workers suggest that the North American findings should not be taken as representative of the level of eating morbidity in Middle Europe (Neumärker *et al.* 1992).

The differences were initially attributed to variable diagnostic practices than true cultural differences between Europe and the USA. Early epidemiological research did not in fact concern itself with any possible cultural differences within Europe or indeed between Europe and the USA. Both Europe and the USA belonged to the white western culture and therefore the bulk of the early transcultural research was understandably more focused on the *other*, i.e. inter-racial differences.

The issue of cultural differences between the USA and Europe was first raised when fourteen European exchange students developed their eating disorder after arriving in the USA. The different environment was suggested to be a precipitating factor, and there was even reference to a possible 'culture clash' (Van Den Brouke and Vandereycken 1986).

Subsequent studies attempted to substantiate these claimed European/American differences in the prevalence of eating disorders. American students were shown, for instance, to have a higher level of eating disturbances than Spanish; this was thought to be due to different dietary habits between the two countries, besides the fact that obesity in Spain was considered much less of a problem than in the USA (Raich *et al.* 1992). Austrian and American women were also found to differ in their level of satisfaction with their body weight (Mangweth *et al.* 1994).

The differences between the USA and Europe in this context were mirrored by similar differences within Europe itself. The

position of eating disorders research in Europe became more complicated with publications emerging from eastern Europe indicating the occurrence of these syndromes, particularly bulimia, in
those countries.

One interesting study was conducted at the time when Berlin
was still a divided city. Its objective was clearly to see if there
were differences in eating attitudes between girls from East and
West Berlin. The different socio-political systems to which the
two parts of Berlin were subject were thought to be responsible
for the evolution of two distinct societies, despite the fact that the
two Berlins had a shared history. When the comparison was
made between diagnosed cases of anorexia nervosa in East and
West Berlin, the East Berliners showed a lower drive for thinness
and less body dissatisfaction than the West Berlin patients on the
Eating Disorders Inventory (Steinhausen *et al.* 1991). However,
when the comparison was made between non-clinical groups, the
total score on the Eating Attitude Test questionnaire (EAT) for
the East Berlin secondary school sample was significantly higher
than that of their West Berlin counterparts. The performance of
the EAT in the West Berlin group was considered comparable to
that in Britain and Belgium, while its validity was questioned
among the East Berliners. The differences in this study between
East and West Berliners were explained in terms of sociocultural
differences between the two groups. The authors concluded that it
would remain to be seen if these differences would diminish after
reunification (Neumärker *et al.* 1992).

Germany was found on the whole to have lower rates of eating
pathology than North America and other countries in Europe
(Steinhausen 1984, Neumärker *et al.* 1992). When the German
Democratic Republic, Austria and Hungary were compared, Hungary was shown to have the highest rates. The rate for subclinical
bulimia nervosa, for instance, was found to be twice as high as in
the other two countries (Rathner *et al.* 1995). In an earlier study
the rate for bulimia nervosa in Hungary was found to be comparable to figures reported in other western European countries
(1.3 per cent). This may indicate a recent increase in the occurrence of these disorders, which seems to be happening against a
background of prevalent obesity. Being overweight was considered
a risk factor for developing eating disorders in Hungary (Szabo
and Túry 1991).

Table 3.4 Eating disorders in Europe

Country	Author	Source	Findings
Britain	Szmukler (1983), Szmukler et al. (1986), Williams and King (1987)	Hospital records	AN 2–4/100,000
	King (1989), Cooper and Fairburn (1983)	Community studies	AN 1.1% BN 1.1–1.9%
Sweden	Cullburg and Engström-Lindberg (1988)	Hospital records	AN 3.9/100,000 BN 2.6/100,000
Denmark	Joergensen (1992)	Hospital records	AN 11.100,000[a] BN 5.5/100,000
Switzerland	Willi and Grossman (1983), Willi et al. (1990)	Hospital records	1.1/100,000 (↑incidence of bulimic behaviours)
Netherlands	Hoek et al. (1995)	GP records	AN 8.1/100,000 BN 11.5/100,000 (↑incidence of bulimia with urbanization)
Italy	Cuzzolaro (1991)	Community/EAT	AN 0.8% BN 1.0% Subclinical 8%

Country	Reference	Method	Results
France	Ledoux et al. (1991)	Special Q	BN 0.7%–1.3%
Austria/Italy	Rathner and Messner (1993)	Community EAT/ANIS	AN 1.3% Subclinical BN 0.87%
Austria	Rathner et al. (1995)	Community/EDI	BN 0.6% Subclinical BN 1.9%
Germany	Neumärker et al. (1992)	Community/EAT	Significant differences in EAT scores between East and West Berliners
	Rathner et al. (1995)[b]	Community/EDI	BN 0% Subclinical cases 1.7%
Hungary	Szabo and Tury (1991)	Community/EAT	BN 1.3% BN 1% cases
	Rathner et al. (1995)	Community/EDI	Subclinical cases 3.8%
Poland	Włodarczyk-Bisaga (1994)	Community/EAT	BN 2.1%
Czech Republic	Krch (1994)	Community/ Special Q	3–5% Eating morbidity

[a] Differences in the rate of hospitalization between AN and BN
[b] Point prevalence for female population only
AN = anorexia nervosa, BN = bulimia nervosa

A similar picture was also found in Poland, where abnormal eating attitudes, as judged by positive EAT scores, were found to be prevalent in 9 per cent of the Polish student population and 2 per cent were considered to have atypical or partial syndrome of an eating disorder (Włodarczyk-Bisaga, 1994).

The increase in the incidence of anorexia nervosa created a need for a specialized unit in Prague (Faltus 1986). Krch considered it a new problem arising against a background of high levels of obesity and caused by changes and confusion in the living patterns of people in the Czech Republic after political changes. He commented that there are strenuous efforts to accept the new identity, with increased orientation towards external signs of western lifestyle. It was suggested that 3–5 per cent of adolescent Czech girls could be at risk of developing eating disorders despite the fact that the medical profession and health services remain largely uninformed of the problem (Krch 1994). It has been argued that eastern Europe is now experiencing gross economic, social and political changes, with strong identification with western Europe, which could be responsible for this phenomenon (Rathner et al. 1995).

Table 3.4 summarizes the studies of eating disorders in Europe.

MAKING SENSE OF IT ALL

There is no doubt that all these studies clearly show that eating disorders are increasingly becoming a global phenomenon. There are still variabilities in the findings between different studies but all of them point consistently to the emergence of these disorders in all societies worldwide.

There are scientific problems with some of these studies which could possibly affect the degree of confidence in their results. They all share common drawbacks including doubts about the degree to which the samples are representative of the whole community, lack of uniformity of the method used in detecting abnormalities in eating attitudes as well as the use of different diagnostic criteria. The majority of these studies also looked at populations that are very diverse and used ambiguous assessments for their ethnicities. Some were even conducted on second-generation immigrants who were born and educated in a white western culture and yet were still viewed as representing their cultures of origin.

However, the most significant methodological limitation is related to the use of the Eating Attitude Test questionnaire (EAT) which was by far the commonest instrument used in all the studies mentioned. EAT scores were used as a crude index of eating pathology in the majority of these studies.

There are issues related to the performance of the EAT in different socio-economic groups. A clear but inconsistent relationship was found between social class and EAT scores in a number of studies. Contrary to what would be expected, EAT scores were found to decrease with higher social class (Eisler and Szmukler 1985, Nasser 1994a). However, the reverse was true in other studies where individuals drawn from middle-class backgrounds had higher scores on the questionnaire (Neumärker et al. 1992, Turpin 1995). These differences may indeed reflect difficulties in assessing socio-economic classes in different societies, where for instance professional status does not always correlate with the degree of wealth (Nasser 1992).

The main source of criticism, however, stems from the fact that the questionnaire had to be translated into different languages and administered to groups culturally different from the Canadian group on which the EAT was first validated. The EAT was translated into Arabic, Hebrew, Spanish, Italian, German, Japanese, Hindi, Urdu, Hungarian, Polish and others. Its validity was doubted when it was translated into Hindi and Urdu as concern was raised about possible linguistic and conceptual misunderstanding of some of its items (King and Bhugra 1989, Choudry and Mumford 1992). Some of the questions, for instance, were thought to be culturally misconceived, such as 'like my clothes to fit tightly', 'cut my food into small pieces' and 'like to eat my food slowly'. All were thought to attract responses in the anorexic direction for reasons of social desirability (Nasser 1984, Mumford et al. 1991).

However, when attempts were made to properly assess the psychometric properties of the EAT in some of these populations, the results pointed to an overall coherence and reasonable internal consistency among its items, particularly in relation to the dieting factor of the questionnaire (Mumford et al. 1991, Nasser 1994b, Mukai et al. 1994).

The reservation raised against the use of the EAT in different cultural groups was useful in drawing attention to the need to improve the current methods used in transcultural research in this area. It has been suggested that future studies should be undertaken within the context of multicentre collaboration between research workers from different cultures and settings. These studies should be able to address the interaction between cultural factors and socio-economic variables and include other relevant issues such as body satisfaction, dietary practices and value orientation. There is also a strong need for proper assessment of family structures and parent–child relationships in other cultures (Pate *et al.* 1992).

Despite limitations, these studies have nonetheless contributed greatly towards the debate on the cultural determinism of eating pathology since they have indicated that these disorders are no longer confined to one particular society or culture. The main findings of these studies can be summarized as follows:

1 Eating pathology, a condition initially thought to be unique to white western cultures, is now emerging in societies/races/cultures that were for a long time presumed immune to this pathology, and possibly occurs with similar or even higher rates to those reported in the West.
2 The incidence and prevalence of eating disorders in the USA are greater than in Europe. This is seen to reflect genuine cross-cultural differences with particular reference to the style of food consumption and the prevalence of obesity in the USA.
3 There is evidence of intra-European variations in the extent and nature of eating pathology. The rates seem to be relatively high in Britain and particularly low in Germany. More significant, however, are the differences between eastern and western Europe, where there is an indication that eating disorders that were largely unreported before are now on the increase in eastern Europe. Bulimia, which was thought to be virtually unknown in eastern Europe before the political changes, is now likely to be the commonest variety.
4 The global emergence of eating pathology in the majority of societies is linked to the degree of identification with western cultural norms in relation to weight and shape preferences for women. The global media could possibly be playing an important role in disseminating these values. The phenomenon was also related to increased rates of obesity worldwide, possibly subsequent to changes in dietary habits. All of this, as well as

the impact of immigration, family pathology and intergenerational conflicts, merits further discussion and analysis.

Family pathology, migrational stress and intergenerational conflicts

A significant proportion of the cases of eating disorders reported among those from non-western ethnicities seem to highlight the presence of family pathology, particularly intergenerational conflicts and confusion over racial identity.

The role of the family in generating eating pathology has long been seen as a fundamental aspect of the psychodynamic approach to this problem. The emphasis on the importance of the family is to be found in Lasègue's early description of the syndrome of anorexia nervosa:

> It must not cause surprise to find me thus always placing in parallel the morbid condition of the patient and the preoccupations of those who surround her. These two circumstances are intimately connected and we should acquire an erroneous idea of the disease by confining ourselves to an examination of the patient . . . the moral medium amid which the patient lives, exercises and influences would be regrettable to overlook or misunderstand.
>
> (Lasègue 1873)

Difficulty in adapting to change, rigidity of thinking and over-protectiveness were some of the family features that were thought to breed psychosomatic disorders. Under these circumstances the illness seems to exercise – rather paradoxically – a stabilizing role in maintaining the unity of the family. In these families, proximity operates within a framework of weak boundaries between its individuals, where protection flourishes at the expense of autonomy and self-realization (Minuchin et al. 1978). Bruch described the anorexic girl as having no control: 'Such a child does not feel she is living her own life, but feels deprived of inner guide posts like being the property of her parents' (Bruch 1978). The anorexic's food refusal could then be seen as an attempt to assert her own identity within her family's pathological framework.

The family's façade of unity hides behind it a lot of anger and resentment which is never expressed for fear of open conflicts leading to poor conflict resolution. Conflicts are avoided for the sake of maintaining this outer image of happiness. This is commonly facilitated by the power schism that exists in these families, with the father being perceived as the weaker partner who easily gives in to the mother's unreasonable demands and manipulations (Selvini-Pallazoli 1974, Minuchin *et al.* 1978).

Families in other cultures were thought possibly to have different structures and also different interactions that lower their vulnerability to psychosomatic disorders, including eating disorders. However, this is not really the case. In one study where the Minuchin model was adopted to assess the Egyptian families' dynamics in relation to asthmatic children, the finding confirmed the presence of similar patterns of behaviour among Egyptian families to those described in western families (Hassan 1995).

One of the other commonly held theories is that non-western families operate within the extended family model, which should theoretically guard against all the drawbacks of the nuclear family. However, in reality the notion of the extended family is now considered in many non-western societies a legacy of the past – a kind of luxury that most societies cannot afford, with increased urbanization, social mobility and migration to the cities or indeed abroad for education or work. It is true to say that the nuclear family is the norm among city dwellers in the majority of societies today, and family ties are clearly loosening under the pressure of modern life. There is also increasing rejection by the younger generations of the concept of extended family, which is seen as obstructive to the emergence of one's own individuality and is also regarded as impeding progress through its emphasis on tradition. There is no doubt that the preservation or the abandonment of the extended family model is closely related to the degree of urbanization and modernization within any given society. The degree of urbanization, as mentioned before, was shown to be associated with increased vulnerability to eating disorders.

It is significant that eating disorders research carried out on populations that originated from the Indian subcontinent and living in the UK drew attention to the possible role played by the family in generating this problem. It was suggested that Indian girls from traditional backgrounds were more at risk of developing eating disorders. These girls were found to face real conflicts in their attempt to adjust to a culture that is different from their parents' (Mumford *et al.* 1991). The issue of the culture conflict or clash is not seen as separate from the issue of racism. It is regarded more as a reflection of a conflict between colour and culture rather than a real conflict between two cultures. Asian adolescents in Britain perceive rejection and lack of acceptance by society of their Britishness, because of colour, which in turn increases their conflict with their parents because they see them as the source of their predicament. The more discrepancy there is between the family's appearance – i.e. dress, language, lifestyle – and that of the young Asian, the more the conflict (Parekh 1983).

In view of the vagueness of the concept of cultural conflicts, perceived parental control was used instead as an index of family pathology. A higher level of perceived maternal control in Asian families explained the more prevalent bulimic attitudes among the Asian girls compared with the Caucasians (Ahmad et al. 1994). This perceived maternal control was stronger among the older girls, who were likely to find it interfering with their autonomy (McCourt and Waller 1995).

Maternal overprotectiveness was also found in Japan to possibly increase girls' predisposition to eating pathology (Takahashi et al. 1991). In another study in Japan the mother's criticism towards her daughter's weight was found to increase the latter's vulnerability to eating disturbances (Mukai et al. 1994). Other parental factors in Japanese society that were connected to the occurrence of eating disorders included paternal absence from home for work reasons (Takagi et al. 1991).

Exposure to different value systems in connection to weight and feminine beauty through migration was seen as responsible for increasing one's susceptibility to eating disorders (Fichter et al. 1983, Nasser 1988). Migrational stress and the need to adapt to a new society, where perhaps identification with some of this new society's values is necessary, was considered a vulnerability factor for the development of eating disorders among immigrants (Bulik 1987, Kope and Sack 1987).

The role of cultural changes and intergenerational conflicts in relation to psychopathology was explored in Kuwait, one of the wealthy, oil-producing Gulf states. The Arab Gulf is composed of six states: Saudi Arabia, Oman, Bahrain, Kuwait, the United Arab Emirates and Qatar. All share similar characteristics of small populations, oil-dominated economies and monarchical systems of government. The outstanding feature of the Kuwaiti society, in common with other Gulf states, is the fact that foreign workers tend to outnumber the native population. These foreign

workers arrive there with their own cultural loading, a phenomenon commonly referred to as 'acculturation in reverse'. Other
features include the rapid acquisition of wealth and prosperity
and subsequent rapid modernization. This has brought with it
increased exposure to western values, cross marriages and the
importation of foreign nannies. The impact of these nannies on
the new generation is yet to be explored. All these changes were
happening, however, while the society was still functioning within
traditional frameworks of marriages and family structures.

Interparental and intergenerational conflicts were found to be
prevalent in this society. The conflicts were seen to be between
this society's indigenous culture and the imported cultures. More
liberal attitudes, lower age and a small education gap between the
parents minimized these conflicts. The parents who had these
characteristics were often of non-Kuwaiti origin and had been
exposed to a gradual process of westernization in the communities
they came from, like Egypt and Jordan. On the other hand, these
conflicts were more likely to occur among parents of Kuwaiti
origin and were more widespread in urban than in Bedouin
areas, highlighting again the role of urbanization (El-Islam *et al.*
1988).

Another important aspect which could have significant impact
on family structure is the absence of the father or both parents
by reasons of working abroad. There is a tendency for some
parents, as is the case with some Egyptian families, to leave their
children behind to be brought up by grandparents or indeed to
decide to send them back home when they reach a certain age to
live with the grandparents. Ironically, this tends to take place at a
crucial age: namely, when the children are at the level of secondary
school education. The decision to be left with the grandparents is
occasionally instigated by the teenagers themselves, in pursuit of
greater freedom than is perhaps allowed in the societies where
their parents work. However, in the majority of cases it is the
parents' decision, made in the belief that their children could possibly have better chances of getting to university if they received
their secondary school education in their own country. Apparently
no research has been done to explore the effect of this peculiar
family structure on the children's psychological health. It can
only be expected that it is likely to escalate the intergenerational
conflicts and in turn increase their propensity to psychopathology.

Wealth and poverty

One of the theories that has long been put forward to explain the perceived protection of other cultures from the development of eating disorders is the fact that they are not rich enough to develop a disorder often associated with wealth. Leff (1988) suggested in his book, *Psychiatry round the Globe*, that if eating disorders are linked to the degree of affluence of any society, the oil-producing countries ought to be an obvious site for the occurrence of these syndromes.

However, the argument is not just about money. The impact of oil wealth on the Gulf was followed by an accelerated development. The process of modernization, that was possibly spread over nearly a century in other Arab states, was compressed into two decades in the Gulf region. So while these countries appear on the surface as highly modernized, they remain underneath very traditional, which led to tremendous social upheaval and cultural imbalance. This, perhaps far more than sheer affluence, is likely to increase this region's individuals' vulnerability to psychological disturbances, including eating disorders.

Wealth is not only limited to the Gulf states; there are wealthy sectors in many countries that have developing economies, such as India or Egypt. There is for instance in Egypt a significant proportion of society that acquired considerable wealth in recent years either through employment in the Gulf states or through liberalization of the economy. The emphasis has increasingly been on the display of wealth, in every aspect of life but notably in food consumption, designer clothes and the ownership of expensive cars and properties in exclusive resorts on the Mediterranean or the Red Sea. Many of these changes have been linked to the transition from state-controlled to free-market economy – perhaps a similar picture to what is now perceived in eastern Europe and the old Soviet Union. In an article in a women's magazine (*Marie Claire* 1995) the reporter examined the growing number of millionaires in Russia after the fall of communism. This phenomenon resulted in a new generation of 'plump' girls who were described as having strong feminine character! These children have everything, from designer clothes, private schools where they eat five meals a day, to bodyguards who protect them from the envy of their poorer neighbours!

The increased predisposition to eating pathology was often found in affluent families, where the child took centre stage and a display of good parenting became almost a sign of social status:

> It is generally believed that the basic transformation of the family has been the rise of children to the position of central importance in the home after centuries of neglect . . . before, there was no social prestige to be derived from being a good parent and none to be lost by being a bad one.
>
> (Selvini-Pallazoli 1985)

Hence, one of the aspects of displaying wealth is increased parental attention and protectiveness towards their children, with too much emphasis placed on their nutrition, which could lead to an early onset of obesity. Early onset obesity has been shown to lead to the development of distorted body image and a predisposition to developing eating disorders (Stunkard 1959). It is interesting that in Egypt the children whose parents work in the Gulf are often caricatured as 'fat children who wear eye glasses'; their obesity is ascribed to excess food consumption and their poor eyesight to watching too much television!

The issue of wealth and poverty in relation to eating pathology was explored in American society, where a connection was made between teenage pregnancy and anorexia nervosa. Both are seen as an exercise in control of female sexuality, and the two expressions are moulded by socio-economic differences. Teenage pregnancy is an affirmation of sexuality by the deprived adolescent who has no other source of power (Brumberg 1988).

In the same vein, hysteria, which is seen as having possibly been replaced by anorexia nervosa in developed societies, is still alive and well in other societies. Many of these societies are still perceived as sexually repressive, a condition that is likely to increase with the increase in puritanical tendencies associated with the recent rise in religious fundamentalism. There is a link between the evolution of religious fundamentalism and economic difficulties, an issue that will be discussed later. It is possible therefore to envisage that, in non-western societies, hysteria will continue to be the expression of distress among women from poorer socio-economic backgrounds, while eating disorders will possibly become the presentation of the relatively rich.

The McDonald's culture – importing new diet

The relationship between the importance of food in any culture and the increased predisposition to eating pathology was argued by Rowland (1970), who thought that the Jewish and the Italians were more at risk of developing eating disorders because of the emphasis their respective cultures place on food.

However, in many non-western societies, food occupies a very special place in the culture and many of the social interactions revolve around food. The Indians and the Chinese have their varied and rich cuisines. The Chinese have been described as being preoccupied with food, and offering good food is seen as means of showing affection, to the extent that some Chinese would say 'have you eaten?' as a form of greeting when others would say 'Hello'. According to Confucianism, human nature has an innate desire for food and sex, which needs to be satisfied. Chinese food has balanced qualities consisting of cold (yin) and hot types (yang) following the principles of Chinese philosophy (Lee *et al.* 1989).

Food also dominates Arab social life; hospitality is a highly appreciated quality and the standards of hospitality are tradition-ally determined and strictly observed (Hamadi 1960). It is interest-ing that the Arab physician Avicenna was able to point as early as the eighth century to the dangers of eating to excess: 'for a meal is injurious when it brings fullness as wine is injurious if it exceeds moderation' (cited in Gruner 1930). Food in the Arab world has been the subject of many influences: Greek, Italian, Turkish and French. In Egypt, bread, commonly wholemeal, stands out as being the most important component of the Egyptian diet. The expression used by the Egyptians to refer to the bond of living together or sharing life (Ishra) is having eaten bread together. Pulses, grains and a wide variety of vegetables and fruits have been standard since ancient times. Lamb is the main meat in the Arab world, commonly served grilled on charcoal (Kebab) with rice, a dish which was introduced to the Arab world by the Turks. In common with other Mediterranean societies, they have a rich repertoire of desserts, mainly flaky pastry and sorbets (Roden 1989).

However, many countries in the non-western world have under-gone changes in their dietary habits, through the introduction of the fast food chains selling beefburgers and fried chicken. Robert-son (1992) mentioned that the McDonald's restaurants have directly influenced the quality and choice of food available in highly urbanized western society. Much of the difference in the rates of eating disorders between Europe and the USA has been blamed on the American style of food consumption, with particular reference to the fast food industry. The same feature has already extended to other societies. In Japan the impact of the McDonald's culture on the traditional Japanese style of eating has been recognized, with beefburgers beginning to replace boiled rice and fish. A link was made between this change in diet and the emergence of eating pathology (Nogami *et al.* 1984).

The appearance of fast food in Chinese society, with its higher fat and sugar content and low fibre, has been predicted to create a problem with obesity which could consequently induce a state of weight consciousness in a society that is now considered at least relatively free from this problem (Lee *et al.* 1989).

The fast food industry is also spreading rapidly in Egypt, with several branches of McDonald's throughout Cairo. It is gradually becoming more popular, especially among the young, than the authentic vegetarian falafel sandwich, despite the difference in cost. The susceptibility of any society to changes in eating habits is demonstrated in how children change their food preferences secondary to social influences, particularly from other peer children. Fictional heroes were also found to be effective agents of this social transmission (Birch 1980).

White bread has also replaced the traditional wholemeal bread, and ironically television advertisements have started to convey the message of the need to 'sprinkle bran over food'. Another addition to the American food choices in Egypt is the Baskin Robbins ice cream chain, which is extremely popular because it is claimed to be less fattening!

The spread of the McDonald's culture acquired a political significance when the first branch opened in Moscow. There was a kind of parallelism between Glasnost and McDonald's. It was the final symbol of the triumph of the American culture and the ending of the cold war. Observers commented on the fact that the McDonald's queue was longer than that for Lenin's mausoleum, at a time when Lenin's name was still cherished by the Soviet public. The McDonald's message spread to the whole of eastern Europe, where its famous sign became a recognizable signal of the opening to the West.

Obesity – rejected

The change in dietary habits has been associated with changes in lifestyle, marked by reduced activity, particularly after the mechanization of domestic work. All of this was behind the recent increase in average weight. The rise in weight consciousness and the increased incidence of eating disorders did in fact take place against this increase in average weight norms, particularly for women (Garner *et al.* 1980).

Premorbid obesity is noted in a significant proportion of anorexics and has been a common finding in some of the reports and studies mentioned in this chapter. The increased prevalence of obesity in non-western societies is associated with increased food consumption, which has taken place as a consequence of social and economic changes.

The propensity to obesity in women was significantly found to be directly related to how early or late menarchial age was: the earlier the menarche the more likely that women will run the risk of obesity (Crisp 1967). An early menarchial age is common in a number of non-western societies, particularly in the Middle East (Nasser 1992). This was not the case, however, in China, where it was reported that girls reach their menarche at a later date than their western counterparts, adding another explanation to the apparent rarity of eating disorders in China up till now (Lee *et al.* 1989).

An increase in food consumption is also related to individual psychological factors; people tend to overeat in response to disappointment, emotional tension, loneliness and boredom. Overeating to combat feelings of boredom, sadness or frustration is a common problem for a lot of people (Ruderman 1985). Food seems to act as a substitute gratification which ameliorates an unpleasant or intolerable life situation: 'A woman who feels out of control cannot reach her body signals of hunger or fullness' (Lawrence 1987). This use or abuse of food for emotional reasons was summed up in Bruch's statement 'I have come to the conclusion that, for many, obesity has an important positive function, it is a compensatory mechanism in a frustrating and stressful life' (Bruch 1966).

In the Czech Republic, 30 per cent of the population was reported to be threatened by obesity, probably because of excess consumption of unsuitable food. This increased rate of obesity was associated with increase in the concern with weight, which led women to pursue dieting (Krch 1995).

Binge eating was also found to be particularly common in the Egyptian population and was closely related to dietary restraint (Dolan and Ford 1991). Binge eating is often considered either a consequence or a precipitant of dietary restraint (Hawkins and Clement 1980, Wardle and Beinhart 1981).

Purging behaviour, considered an early stage of the full syndrome of bulimia nervosa, was also suggested to be a common form of weight control in low-income populations (Martin and Wollitzer 1988). Purging behaviour was found to be more common than vomiting in the reported Chinese cases (Schmidt 1993) and also the black community in the USA (Emmons 1992).

The role of social contagion in causing bulimia is yet another important factor. Some of the cases identified in community studies have been in contact with diagnosed cases (Nasser 1984, Chiodo and Latimer 1983). Recent reports of cases of eating disorders in the kibbutz tend to support this, as the phenomenon was partly attributed to the communal nature of the kibbutz where the girls tended to identify with each other in this respect (Apter et al. 1994).

All these factors explain the reasons behind the finding of bulimia and not anorexia nervosa in the majority of the studies mentioned. However, the most important factor seems to be the degree of prevalence of obesity in any given society. The issue of obesity cannot really be separated from either anorexia or bulimia nervosa. An overlap between the three categories was suggested, with one common underlying feature of dissatisfaction with body weight (Russell 1985).

In Buenos Aires, the drive for thinness and body dissatisfaction was found to be common among obese women. Vulnerability to bulimia increased with an increase in weight and an early onset of obesity (Zukerfeld and Cormillot 1991). The higher the weight among native American women, the higher was the desire to lose weight and even engage in hazardous weight-reducing measures (Rosen et al. 1988).

Aerobics classes, shaping-up centres and health clubs have increased in Egypt in recent years, with proliferation of private weight reduction clinics offering acupuncture or hypnotherapy (Lewnes 1991). It is interesting that in one of the eating disorders studies conducted in Lahore, the authors commented that the

girls appeared to be living in a dieting milieu, with roadside advertisements for slimming clinics and keep-fit clubs seen increasingly
often in the wealthier suburbs of Lahore (Mumford *et al.* 1992).
The increase in the undesirability of fatness seems to be shared by
men, who also apparently want their women to be slimmer.

This dissatisfaction with one's weight, which was once considered absent in non-western societies, is now becoming an
increasingly common problem. The increase in the rates of obesity
in non-western societies appears therefore to be associated with an
increased rejection of obesity.

The global village – the role of the media

The role of the media in promoting the concept of thinness has
been discussed in the first chapter of this book. The contribution
of the media to eating pathology was mainly studied in the West.
The media is seen to present images of thinness through role
models or through images that imply social desirability. By so
doing they increase the chances of identification. Women were
found to use media images as a reference source in evaluating
their own body image and also their sense of acceptance or
approval (Silverstein *et al.* 1986, Anderson and Di Domenico
1992).

Seeing photographs of thin fashion models led to a reduction in
women's general sense of self-esteem (Irving 1990). Other research
confirmed this effect, particularly on adolescent groups (Waller
et al. 1992). Women also appear to be more easily manipulated
by media images than men although there is an indication that
men's self-esteem too is influenced by what is portrayed on the
media (Murphy 1993).

Perhaps the main explanation for the universal spread of the
concept of thinness and the global increase in weight consciousness
is the dissemination of the thinness ideal through mass media. The
role of mass media in shaping and possibly unifying culture today
cannot be underestimated.

The impact of television on the new generation in Japan has
been observed:

the younger generation has grown up in front of the TV set . . .
the modern condition must bear witness to a process by which

it has become less Japanese and hence, we can only conclude, more western.

(Edwards 1989)

It is interesting that in one of the studies carried out in Japan with the intention of assessing the level of eating disorders in this society, the authors speculated that girls who spent a lot of time watching television could potentially increase their susceptibility to eating disorders (Mukai *et al.* 1994).

However, many sections of the western media appeared unconcerned with their influences in other societies. They continued to fail to dispel ignorance about these societies and promoted the same old stereotypes. The majority of non-western societies are often seen in the western media as mainly victims of famines or civil wars. Muslim women are also often portrayed in the image that corresponds to the western fantasy in this respect, i.e. fully covered in black cloaks.

Hollywood movies played a major role too, particularly in depicting a certain image for black women, who have often been portrayed as big and typically played the roles of mammies – the most famous of course in *Gone with the Wind*. In an article in the *Independent* newspaper, Linda Grant asked 'if dieting was a black and white issue'. She reaffirmed the notion that black women regard big as beautiful, contrary to most research findings in this respect. The reason perhaps for her reaching such a conclusion is likely to be that the issue of class was not taken into account. Most of the women she talked to came from the Brixton area and were largely from low socio-economic backgrounds (Grant 1994). This issue has been, in fact, commonly ignored, not only in the popular press but also in scientific epidemiological studies too. The tendency was to attribute any body shape differences between groups to ethnicity, although in reality they were more likely to be a reflection of difference in social class (Ahmad *et al.* 1994).

In other work, black women were shown to be affected to the same extent by the media as white women. This resulted in distorted concepts about their body image and the belief that thinness is equivalent to happiness (Strauss *et al.* 1994). Diet articles were also shown to feature in black magazines, where thinness was seen as a parameter of black achievement and social mobility within the wider (but thinner) American middle class (Schwartz 1986).

The change in the perception of weight among Egyptian women, with evidence of increased dissatisfaction with body weight, was also linked to the amount of American soap opera shown on Egyptian television (Lewnes 1991). Commercial advertising through Egyptian women's magazines started in recent years to take the issue of dieting and thinness on board. There is a specialized magazine that was first issued in 1987 called *El Rashaka* (which means in Arabic slimness) as well as the Arabic versions of the international women's magazines, *Elle* and *Vogue* (Nasser 1992).

The access to western media has considerably increased in recent years through the spread of satellite channels. There is an expansion of global media networks like BBC and CNN virtually to all parts of the world. The Middle East alone now has several satellite channels, the majority of which are funded by individuals and survive mainly on commercials. There is a tendency to adopt the western look and style that is perceived as popular. This is particularly evident in entertainment programmes targeted towards youth. However, there is also an increased awareness of the impact of the West on Middle Eastern societies, with many of the serious programmes dedicated to discussing this issue. There is nonetheless a high degree of ambivalence about this influence which is at times seen as desirable and beneficial and at other times a real threat to authentic cultural values or even a form of cultural imperialism.

In an attempt to explore this issue, a small pilot study was carried out on a diverse population of students from different nationalities. The students were drawn from an international hostel in Essen, Germany. This hostel attracts university students from all over the world as part of an international project of university student exchange. Almost all nationalities were represented as well as the three major religions – Judaism, Christianity and Islam – but students from the Indian subcontinent were absent. A specially designed questionnaire covering certain cultural concepts was administered to all students. The items of the questionnaire were intended to cover concepts related to religion, family structure, achievement orientation and the need for group affiliation as opposed to asserting one's own individuality.

Two groups emerged: one with adherence to what is commonly regarded as western values and another slightly distant from it. The majority group (65 per cent) was closely adherent to so-called western values. The membership of this group was heterogeneous and included individuals who would normally be regarded as non-western by virtue of nationality or religion. There was also a consensus view among the students that the world is becoming one by reasons of mass media and information technology.

These results tentatively show that the western value system is likely to be the general value system adopted by the majority of student populations all over the world regardless of their religious or nationality backgrounds (Nasser and Abrams in press). It is interesting that the universality of weight consciousness seemed more apparent in student populations. The majority of the studies discussed in this chapter were carried out on student populations and consistently showed that this particular segment of any society now appears to be generally more at risk of developing eating disorders.

All of this goes to show that increasingly the world is becoming homogeneous through adopting a uniform culture that is determined by both the media and information technology.

Chapter 4

The other women – immune or vulnerable?

EATING DISORDERS – A WOMAN'S DISEASE

From the original description of the syndrome of anorexia nervosa, one can easily see the emphasis that was put on its peculiarity to young women:

> The subjects of this affliction are mostly of the female sex and chiefly between the ages of 16 and 23 . . . and it will be admitted that young women at the ages named are specially obnoxious to mental perversity.
>
> (Gull 1868)

Since then, there has been enough evidence from research and clinical observations to support this notion, which raised the question of what it is in being a woman that constitutes a vulnerability to a disorder that has a great incidence at this particular time in history. This raises certain issues concerning the current position of women that are vital to our sociocultural debate on eating disorders.

In simplistic terms the symptomatology of anorexia nervosa revolves around body fat and menstruation. This body fat has the tendency to concentrate in certain areas of the woman's body that have sexual significance, like the breasts and hips, and a threshold of body fat is an essential requisite for menstruation. Women throughout history were commonly seen through these symbols that stress their biological and sexual functions: 'The female is more enslaved to the species than the male . . . her animality is more manifest' (de Beauvoir 1972).

The relationship between woman's appetite and her own sexuality is a rather old one. In Victorian England, for instance, the

woman's appetite was seen, in the same way as her sexuality, to
demand control:

> young women caught up in the process of sexual maturation
> were subject to vagaries of appetite and peculiar cravings. . . .
> The rapid expansion of the passion and the mind often renders
> the tastes and appetites capricious.
>
> (cited in Brumberg 1988)

The most symbolic of all food was meat, excess meat eating was
linked to adolescent insanity and nymphomania. Women who ate
meat were regarded as acting out of place and assuming a male
prerogative: 'If there is any tendency to precocity in menstruation,
or if the system is very robust and lethoric, the supply of meat
should be quite limited' (cited in Brumberg 1988). Hence, meat
avoidance at the table became the manner of 'proper' women.

In Moravia's novel *1934*, this connection is eloquently illus-
trated in his description of Truade:

> She proved her hunger was not only a boost, inspired perhaps
> by her rivalry with her sister, who was frugal to the point of
> fasting. She ate a lot and, what struck me even more, she ate
> the same course twice, just as in the boat she had wanted to
> make love twice.
>
> (Moravia 1985)

This sexual symbolism of food was taken up by the psychoanalytic
school of thought in its attempt to understand the nature of the
anorexic syndrome. Central to Crisp's theory is the symbolic significance of the anorexic's food avoidance, which conveys her fear
of growing up. This fear is of the normal functioning adolescent
weight, pointing to her desire to stay within the confines of the
greater security and comfort of childhood. By so doing she rejects
her own sexuality and aborts the emergence of her full womanhood (Crisp 1977). This is echoed in Sheila MacLeod's description
of her own anorexic experience: 'It seemed obvious to me at the
time to be a child was safer and easier than to be an adult and
that specifically to be a girl was safer than to be a woman'
(MacLeod 1981).

It has been argued that this biological definition of the woman
has been responsible for limiting her human potential by confining
her over the years to the domestic circle while men had the autonomy and freedom to generate culture by creating values and ideals.

This made women concern themselves more with appearances and heightened their self-consciousness (Ortner 1974). Looking attractive has always been an important criterion for a woman to feel good about herself and also feel accepted (Wooley and Wooley 1984). This has possibly made women more susceptible than men to manipulations by external ideas and images.

In an interesting paper entitled 'To be or not to be a woman', the author argued that anorexia nervosa should be re-categorized as a gender disorder. She finds support for her argument in the degree of discomfort the anorexic feels about her own sexual identity, and the ambivalence she experiences about embracing or rejecting femininity (Mahowald 1992). Women with eating disorders were found to lack a solid sense of sex role orientation and this ambiguity was considered responsible for their reduced self-esteem (Lewis and Johnson 1985).

It has also been suggested that the predicament of the anorexic girl stems from her attempt to achieve successful femininity, while realizing at the same time that these feminine stereotypes are in conflict with the traits that are needed for success. These traits – indifference, assertiveness, autonomy and independence – are characteristic of the male gender and are clearly in contradiction with the presumed feminine qualities of nurturence, deference and affiliation to other people, where the woman's sense of value becomes so dependent upon the approval of others (Orbach 1986).

In keeping with this notion, girls with vulnerability to the development of eating disorder were found to have failed to develop those masculine traits that are necessary for optimal adult female functioning in contemporary society (Sitnick and Katz 1984). They internalized instead the cultural standards of successful femininity to ensure approval and avoid rejection (Boskind-Lodahl 1976, Weeda-Mannak et al. 1990). It is not surprising therefore to find anorexic women to be less liberated in their attitudes and behaviours than the non-anorexic ones, and even when their attitudes appeared somewhat liberated, this was not reflected in their behaviours (Rose et al. 1982).

Despite the anorexic girl's failure to internalize the masculine traits that are necessary for success, they nonetheless continued to be seen and described as achievement oriented: 'There is a peculiar contradiction – everybody thinks you are doing so well and everybody thinks you are great, but your real problem is that you think that you are not good enough' (cited in Bruch 1988).

The girl's desire to achieve is not really separate from the characteristic feminine pleasing orientation. The anorexic girl performs for others, she is not doing it for herself; she is after the applause, seeking approval and affirmation of her own worth and value. This desire to please others or live up to others' expectations explains why a significant proportion of anorexic girls tend to come from families who place an enormous value on success and achievement.

In the anorexic girl's pursuit of success she discovers that her desire to please others is not enough to achieve success. This is what creates the anorexic dilemma and indeed the dilemma of so many women in our modern times. In *The Art of Starvation*, Sheila MacLeod speaks of her own conflict:

> On the one hand we were encouraged to be young ladies, polite, modest and considerate to others – a perfect training for a housewife. On the other hand the school aped the traditions of the boys' public schools, encouraging competitiveness and aggressiveness within a rigidly hierarchical structure.

> (MacLeod 1981)

It is this conflict between the socialized femininity that is needed for social approval and the masculinity required to perform well that sums up the anorexic dilemma:

> The anorexics are aware of two selves that are in constant conflict, one a dominating male self that represents greater spirituality, intellectuality and will power, the other a female that represents uncontrollable appetite and flaws.

> (Bruch 1978)

The socialization process, based on gender distinctions, is bound to affect girls at the time of their adolescence. There is a clear need for the adolescent girl to establish a sense of personal identity, to accept the maturational biological changes that are happening to her and to have a strong desire to please and be accepted by others. It is also to be expected that the degree of identification of the daughter with her mother will determine how successful her socialization and the assimilation of the feminine traits will be.

This formed the basis for the extensive research into the relationship between the anorexic girl and her mother, where it was found that the anorexic girl experiences peculiar differentiation problems from her mother. It is as if she sees her own body as 'the maternal object, from which her ego tries to separate by all means' (Selvini-Pallazoli 1974).

It has also been argued that at the heart of the daughter's problems is a sense of guilt over her mother's condition. The girl sees her mother's life as having been unfulfilled, in contrast to her own situation where she is now presented with new opportunities for fulfilment. The struggle to grow and separate from her mother, in order to achieve her own identity, is perceived to be at the expense of the mother. The fear of anger towards her mother is then displaced onto food and eating, simply because of the primal association between mother and food (Chernin 1986).

The relationship between the new societal expectations of women and eating pathology has been explored by a number of feminist writers. Orbach argues that the thinness ideal is now being imposed on women by society because of the threat to society from the new woman. It is an attempt to hinder and abort her emerging assertiveness and her desire for equality. If women achieve this thinness they metaphorically become less visible or take up less space, which society wants. However, if they hold on to their fat, they may show their anger, rebellion and defiance (Orbach 1978).

The same notion is expressed by Chernin, who highlights the contradictions or the double messages that confront women: 'Women these days are expected to expand and enlarge their possibilities, but also shrink in their bodies, become smaller and petite' (Chernin 1981). The new woman is expected to be a mother, have a career, be a dutiful wife, an exciting mistress, be romantic but also be independent and remain in control of all these (Dolan 1994). These roles came to be known as the superwoman syndrome. Women who internalized the superwoman ideal and wanted to fulfil both male and female stereotypical gender roles were the ones who apparently ran the risk of having eating disorders (Steiner-Adair 1986, Timko *et al.* 1987).

In *The Beauty Myth*, Naomi Wolf focuses on the cultural notion of beauty that reduces the woman to a mere beautiful image. Society allows women to have either mind or body but not both. Beauty, she argues, is a quality that women want to possess, and men want to possess, women who have it. She nonetheless reaffirms that the female's obsession with dieting is more of an obsession with obedience than with beauty itself (Wolf 1990).

And yet, the anorexic is not just an obedient girl; she rebels through conformity, or rejects the pressures by rejecting her own body and by becoming ill. This anorexic stance is seen as a form of hunger strike. Like the hunger striker, she has taken as her weapon a refusal to eat. Not eating is her survival tool (Orbach 1986).

In her obstinate pursuit of thinness, she seems to be trying hard to conform to her prescribed gender role, and yet by developing the final anorexic boy-like look, she is conveying the opposite message. The desire to be ultra-thin was arguably seen as a desire to be desexualized and hence no longer seen as a woman (Selvini-Pallazoli 1974) – a condition referred to as a purge of femaleness (Gordon 1990). The non-fertile look of extreme thinness states a kind of non-reproductive sexuality that is seen as sexually liberating, demanding from society that it value women independently from their reproductive qualities (Bennett and Gurin 1982).

The feminist use of the anorexic position as a metaphor for rebellion has been debated on the basis that the anorexic in her pursuit of thinness does not appear to be that calculating, i.e. aware of the ultimate result of her starvation which is stripping her anatomy and terminating her menstruation (Di Nicola 1988b).

The following points crystallize the debate about the gender specificity of eating disorders.

1 Women are more at risk of eating disorders because fat is an integral part of their own biology.
2 The pursuit of thinness seems to be an active denial of this biology in an attempt by the woman to be respected and valued outside her sexual reproductive capacity.
3 Women who are at risk of developing eating pathology appear to socialize the traditional feminine qualities and fail to have the necessary masculine traits that are required for success.
4 Women are in conflict over gender roles; they do not know whether to remain in their traditional gender role of dependence, attractiveness, and derivation of their self-value from others' approval or to adopt the winning masculine gender of aggressiveness, assertiveness and high achievement. Thinness seems to offer an illusory resolution to this conflict by providing a perfect synthesis of feminine and masculine gender stereotypes.

5) Women who are most at risk of eating disorders are those who expect of themselves to be fulfilling the role of the 'super-woman'.

The issue of gender and eating disorders has been the subject of several publications and is only tackled here as a framework to apply to the case of women from other cultures. It has been highlighted that one of the weaknesses of the feminist argument in this respect is that it failed to address the issue of feminism in its wider cultural context and deal with the position of women in other societies (Di Nicola 1988a).

THE CASE OF THE OTHER WOMEN

These gender-specific issues of eating disorders have commonly been discussed in connection with the position of women in the western industrialized world. The conflict over gender role was seen as a predicament specific to western women and it was thought that women in other cultures were relatively protected from such conflicts by virtue of well-defined sex roles and the preservation of old traditional values in relation to women's place in society.

As discussed in the previous chapter, the thinness ideal has clearly permeated other cultures, and subsequently the syndromes of eating disorders started to emerge. There is a need therefore to start to look at the *other* women and examine the common stereotypes that presume their immunity in this respect.

Who are the other women? Before answering this question, there is a need to examine the basis on which the whole body of trans-cultural research is built. The fundamental approach in transcultural research was to divide the world into simply West (Occident) and East (Orient). The West is normally equated with progress and modernity and the East with stagnation and tradition. The Orient in this case includes all the people and races outside Europe and North America. So by definition the other women are simply the women of the Orient. In the eyes of the westerner the Orient assumed more or less a homogeneous entity despite the wide diversity of the people and the nations that are included in its remit. The concept of the Orient still meant different things to different people; for instance in the USA the likelihood is that the Orient will be more associated with the Far East, although in reality the term was born out of the European contact with the Near East (the Middle East). The historical development of the concept of the Orient has been the subject of a scholarly work by Edward Said (1978), and the intricacies of this complicated issue are clearly outside the scope of this book. The concern here is with the position of women in these societies and the stereotypes that are attached to their gender roles. The assumption, however, is that the position of these women has been rather static and generally unaffected by historical forces.

WOMEN OF THE FAR EAST

Indian subcontinent

In his book *Women and Power in History*, De Riencourt argues that the predominance of the female principle in the Hindu tradition stems from the worship of the divine mother (Matris); she is the earth goddess with a plant sprouting from her womb. The cult of the mother is a major force in Indian culture; all female deities were considered under this great power, the great mother, the ruler of the world.

Women in Vedic India appear to have occupied a high position in society and enjoyed the freedom to choose their mates, a position that was strengthened during the Gupta reign (De Riencourt 1983). This positive attitude towards women changed somewhat in post-Vedic India. Their freedom was increasingly curtailed and they began to be seen as unfit for education: 'for a woman to study the Vedas, indicates confusion of the realm' (Montagu and Loring-Brace 1977).

Women were expected to wear veils and were not allowed to inherit property. The widows were discouraged from remarriage, and the practice of suttee (burning of a widow on the funeral pyre of her husband) was honoured. Other sources of discomfort in relation to women's position in India have been the preservation of the caste system, the tradition of arranged marriages, and the dowry that is needed for the prospective husband, which increased the family's rejection of baby girls.

In Buddhism, the importance given to the female principle earlier in Hinduism began to be undermined. In the Buddhist tradition women are only allowed to be Sisters if they abandon women's thoughts and cultivate the thoughts of man: 'Am I a woman in such matters or I am a man or what am I then . . . verily all such vanities now no more may delight me' (Dubois 1928).

Hinduism had a freer and more natural attitude to sex and emphasized the husband's obligations towards his wife in this respect (Campbell 1962). In the Indian tradition the woman seems to oscillate between some sexual freedom enshrined by religion and its ultimate goal of purity and asceticism. This has strong relevance to our argument since there is a recognized association between anorexia nervosa and asceticism. Buddha is said to have acquired an enormous power and appeal in fasting:

> Then I remember the time when I was a youth at home . . . I was without sexual desires, without evil ideas . . . then there arose in my consciousness that this was the way to enlightenment . . . and then I thought it is not easy to gain that happy state while my body is emaciated.
>
> (Mogul 1980)

It is interesting that the earliest report of a case resembling anorexia nervosa in India was named the Ascetic syndrome (Neki 1973).

Islam in India has probably been influenced by the pre-existing Hindu and Buddhist traditions. It is important to note that, at variance with the Hindu tradition, women in Islam have the right to inherit, and the dowry (*Mahr*) system is quite the reverse: i.e. the woman gets the dowry, not the man.

Another important aspect of Indian culture is the influence of British rule on the status of women in India. Some efforts are known to have been made towards fighting the caste system and the practice of Suttee, which was made illegal in 1829. However, the only evidence for an organized women's movement in India is to be found in women's struggle against the British, and the woman's cause was promoted by Ghandi: 'Woman is the companion of man gifted with equal mental practice, to call the woman the weaker sex is a libel, it is man's injustice to woman' (cited in Visram 1992). Subsequently, certain legislations were passed with the aim of improving the position of women.

India is known for its conservative spirit, and gender inequalities still persist in education and employment. In recent times, despite this conservatism, women of the Indian subcontinent achieved the highest positions of power: from Indira Ghandi to Benazir Bhuto of Pakistan, Sirimavo Bandaranayake of Sri Lanka and Begum

Khaleda of Bangladesh. Perhaps the notion of woman as the mother of the nation has emerged once more in modern India in a style reminiscent of the enduring Indian cult of the great mother.

De Riencourt (1983), who strongly opposes current feminism, celebrates the Indian conservative nature and sees women as fit only for a traditional role. He nonetheless regards women as possibly able to run the state, as it is not all that different from running a house! He finds that modern feminism puts women in a difficult position as they demand from themselves things they naturally do not have. He is very uncompromising in his attack on women's liberation with its drive towards a decrease in sexual differentiation, which in his opinion will eventually lead to social and cultural death.

China

The concept of the mother earth retained the same stronghold on the Chinese mind; Chinese culture was seen as female-like in its destiny, not expected to regulate or master nature, only to adapt to it. Women's position swung from the strict patriarchal code of Confucianism to the more favourable Taoism. The symbol of the Tao is the geometric interplay between the feminine dark and passive forces (yin) and the light, active masculine (yang). The universe is believed to have been born out of co-operation between the two. The Chinese make full use of this sexual dualism, and emphasize the importance of achieving balance between the two through co-operation. Both the male and female elements are sublimated for the sake of the whole, and individuality is sacrificed for the survival of the family or the clan. Worship of the ancestors and reverence of old age take precedence over sex differences and the rights or the plight of either sex (Weber 1951).

The woman's plight is manifestly seen in certain Chinese customs, such as the old custom of feet binding. There is no doubt that the woman's position in Chinese society was inferior to that of the male and her only definition was through her fertility and her reproductive capacity. The Chinese are said to admire a womanly woman, not a girlish female (De Riencourt 1983).

In recent history, China has been subject to communism. The cultural revolution was aimed at increasing women's power and achieving some form of sexual equality. This was done through undermining the patriarchal Confucian system. The critics of this period see that the cultural revolution did nothing except changing women's slavery to the clan to slavery to the party. In spite of all the criticism attached to this period, there is enough evidence to suggest that communism succeeded in making general improvements in women's conditions, with reference to education, employment and the abolition of certain reactionary customs.

Japan

The principles of Confucianism and the collectivist orientation also govern Japan. The supremacy of the state over the individual citizen is at the heart of this group-oriented patriarchal society, which socializes its members to follow its norms almost unthinkingly. There is even a peculiar Japanese therapeutic technique that increases the individual's awareness of the connectedness of the self to others, which is called the Naikan therapy (Murase 1974).

This appears to be in total contrast to the western notion of the self and the promotion of individuality. After the Second World War, the USA planned to remould Japan into a western democracy; the post-war constitution provided an explicit guarantee of the individual's autonomy, and the process of modernization and industrialization pushed Japan more in this direction.

Now Japan is a technologically advanced and wealthy society and yet the position of its women is still judged by its old tradition. For the western observer the women of Japan continue to be seen through tea ceremonies, flower arranging and the apprenticeship of the geisha. Some of that is still true, with Japanese women continuing to be subordinate to men. In an interesting book called *Modern Japan through its Weddings*, Edwards (1989) quotes what the boss of the groom would normally tell the bride in the wedding ceremony: 'When men go out to work in the world things do not always go their way; when they come home, they wish to have everything their way, so please obey whatever your husband says as though you were a child'!

The great majority in Japanese society still favours the persistence of these gender role differences and inequalities. Most surveys show that it is believed to be best to raise boys in a masculine and girls in a feminine manner.

Women still have unequal opportunity in employment and have access only to jobs that are less secure and lower paying.

Professional women have also less chance to get to the top of their professions, and there are still jobs that are seen as exclusive to the male domain. In a public opinion poll carried out by the prime minister's office the results showed that close to 70 per cent of men would be unwilling to work under a female supervisor. Important also was the fact that the Japanese constitution does not make any special allowances for working women. The matter of harmonizing paid work and family life is left entirely to the women to sort out: 'If women are to continue to work on equal terms with men, women's self awakening is required in such fields as work morale and ethics' (cited in Saso 1990).

Despite these social attitudes, Saso argues that there is a perceived change in the position of women, and the total number of female administrators has doubled since the late 1970s; however, this was made possible by women sacrificing their family and personal lives.

Saso acknowledges the increasing admiration of Japanese companies for the American style of management, with a shift towards individualism. Whether this will have a positive or negative impact on women remains to be seen. What is clear, however, is that major westernizing cultural changes are underway in Japanese society which will certainly have implications for the position of Japanese women (Saso 1990).

WOMEN OF THE MIDDLE EAST

Egypt

Egypt is situated at the meeting point of two continents, Asia and Africa, and not far from Europe by virtue of its position on the Mediterranean. Egypt is associated in the mind of any westerner with one of its greatest ancient achievements, the pyramids. However, the people of Egypt tend to be seen as separate from that past, and very little is actually known of them or of the country they live in. Sullivan says in his book *Women in Egyptian Public Life*

> Having lived and worked in Egypt, I was stimulated by growing awareness of the gap between the Egypt I read about and the Egypt I observed in daily life. The chasm between theory and reality seemed specially serious in the case of women in Egypt; women have been contributors to the creative tension in

Egyptian public life on many issues, but specially regarding gender roles.

(Sullivan 1987)

More attention is given here to the position of Egyptian women, not only for the obvious reason that I am one of them, but also because they represent, in my opinion, a unique paradigm for the position of women across time and social change. They belong to an old civilization that raised its women to a very high position. They were also influenced by the Graeco-Roman tradition that is at the root of the formation of western society, and their conscience was shaped by Judaism and Christianity before Islam. The women of Egypt belong to Africa and also to the Arab Moslem tradition where women are commonly defined through rigid and mostly negative stereotypes, but Egypt was in fact exposed relatively early to major westernizing forces and showed readiness to assimilate these new ideas. This is clearly reflected in its feminist movement which took place around the same time as that of Europe. In recent times Egypt experimented with socialism, and the position of its women was subsequently moulded by this experience. Today it tries to adjust to the new realities of the free-market ideology.

Ancient 'modern' women

In contrast to India and China, the woman in ancient Egypt did not represent mother earth; she was instead heaven (*Nut*) who, through her love with the man earth (*Geb*), gave birth to humanity.

In the Egyptian pantheon women occupied prestigious positions and constituted important deities. The most important of all was Maat, the goddess of law, order, justice, balance and harmony.

The woman as a sacred mother was still honoured in ancient Egypt and is epitomized in the story of Isis, who became pregnant through a visitation by the spirit of her husband Osiris, who was murdered by his brother Set. Isis gave birth to Horus who was seen as the saviour of mankind. Isis remained a strong mother cult in ancient Egypt and had great influence on neighbouring Greek and Roman civilizations. The cult of Isis was gradually replaced by the very similar image of the Virgin Mary in Christian Egypt.

Women in Pharonic times were not only goddesses, but they were also queens, priests, scribes and physicians. In art, women were depicted in statues as seated side by side with man, equal in height, stature and dignity: 'We see the women depicted as often as, if not more than the men . . . it is certain that they must have lived on a footing of greater equality with the men than in any other ancient civilisation' (Robins 1993).

Egypt also had several queens, the most famous being Hatshebsut, Nefertiti and Cleopatra.

Hatshebsut was the first woman to rule Egypt. Little is known about her, except for the significant fact that she always depicted herself as a man and appeared on her monuments having a beard and wearing male costume. This was attributed to a desire on her part to be accepted as a legitimate king. However, this does not explain why her officials on some occasions used masculine pronouns to refer to her and on other occasions used feminine ones.

What is also fascinating about this woman is the fact that she called herself the female Horus, analogous to a woman calling herself today the female Christ. But while she presents herself as a man and refers to herself as the feminine part of God, she still appears happy with her femininity in her identification with Hathor, the goddess of beauty and fertility. Interestingly, her childminder was a man, the same architect who built her famous temple (Robins 1993).

Nefertiti, on the other hand, was a non-ruling queen, the wife of Akhenaten, the heretic king who was behind the Amarna revolution that introduced to Egypt new art and new ways of thinking. Paglia argues in her book *Sexual Personae* that Nefertiti's image captures the very essence of western beauty: 'It is western ego under glass'.

Nefertiti's bust, which is now in the Berlin museum, is regarded as the most popular work of art in the world. Paglia describes her as

half masculine, vampire of political power, futuristic with the enlarged cerebrum foreseen as the destiny of our species. . . . She is an android manufactured being, her femaleness is mathematical, femaleness impersonalised by masculine abstraction. She is beautiful but desexed. Her perfection is for display not use.

(Paglia 1990)

Nefertiti was the elegant beautiful woman, the housewife and the mother. The picture of the couple with their daughters was an early celebration of this apparently happy nuclear family. Paglia clearly traces the roots of contemporary western beauty to Nefertiti's image, where she argues that Egypt had invented femininity to replace femaleness. Everything fat, slack and sleepy is gone: 'She is the epitome of elegance, reduction and condensation . . . exquisite and artificial, she is western personality in its ritual bonds' (Paglia 1990). This resonates with Clark's earlier description of Egyptian art: 'The Egyptian sculptors invented a type of beauty that was so exquisite and delicate it did not appear again in the history of art until Fourteenth Century France and the early Italian renaissance' (Clark 1980).

The position of women in ancient Egypt was said to have shocked the Greeks, and Herodotus commented that women were very liberated in ancient Egypt. On the other hand the majority of scholars have described the position of women in classical Greece as very restricted. Women were not allowed out of the house and were kept in locked *gynaeconities* (women's quarters) where the men never entered. Women hardly presented themselves in public, and it was not appropriate to know a woman's name; her name, like her person, should be shut in the house. Women were advised not to be seen even near a window, and a death penalty awaited women who dared to show themselves at the Olympic games. Women were regarded as a lower order than men, weaker in heart and intellect and incapable of taking part in public life. Women were viewed as either courtesans, concubines or wives whose job was merely to bear lawful offspring (Becker 1866, Rousseau 1960).

Women's legal status deteriorated, and inheritance through the maternal line, which was the rule in ancient Egypt, also disappeared. Legislation went as far as regarding anything done under the influence of women not to be legally binding.

The male-dominated perspective of the world was to continue into Roman times, except for sporadic occasions of rebellion against male authority. Women's rebellion manifested in their despising themselves for being women, looking down on child bearing as unworthy of their talents. Some women even put on men's clothing and cut their hair short, to defeminize themselves (Dill 1925).

This physical identification with the male did not appear to advance their attempt to change the pathetic status of women. Analysts argue that the Roman women's rebellion did not evolve into a significant movement because of its anti-male orientation and because it was marred by the turmoil through which all society was going, with widespread breakdown of religion and authority (De Riencourt 1983).

An example of a woman belonging to the Egyptian tradition and yet living and ruling in a Graeco-Roman period is Cleopatra, the most controversial of all Egyptian queens, who invited both criticism and veneration. Cleopatra's controversy stems more perhaps from the time in which she lived than from her personality. She arrived on the scene when history was at a crossroads and culture was reformulating social prescriptions for gender. Egypt to the Romans at that time, said Paglia, was like Renaissance Italy to mediaeval England (Paglia 1990).

Cleopatra's predicament was the fact that she was too much of a woman and also too much of a man; she appropriated both genders. Her femininity was expressed according to her own rules, not dictated, measured or controlled. Her identification with the male was not new in the Egyptian culture, she was very much like Hatchebsut with whom she liked to identify but also found herself comfortable with the maternal role of Isis, and was often portrayed in her image. The Romans saw her as baffling and could not understand how a woman could be so expressive of her femininity and yet be so manly and aggressive. It is interesting that Anthony was seen by the Romans as effeminate by his association with her.

Women in Islam

It is clear that man's ascent to power and the relegation of women to inferior positions began in Graeco-Roman times. However, this position was arguably enforced by the advent of religion. Religion revolved around morality which was commonly defined by the woman's sexual behaviour. Women in Judaism treated their husbands as their lords, and the wife was almost considered part of her husband's possessions. This is seen in the Talmudic prayer 'O God, let not my offspring be a girl, for very wretched is the life of woman', and added daily, 'Blessed be thou, O Lord our God for not making me a woman' (cited in De Riencourt 1983).

Women's sexuality seems to be at the root of the Jewish discrimination of women which is based on the assumption that women's sexual drive is greater than that of man and that women are seductive beings that lead men into sexual misadventure. That is the reason why they needed to be covered and made as invisible as possible. The theme of women's desire is recurrent in the old testament and the Talmud where, in the talmudic legislation, man should give adequate satisfaction to his wife's sexual requirements.

However, women in Judaism enjoyed a tremendous position of power as mothers; it was almost as if God delegated part of his creative power to them to bear and bring up children (De Riencourt 1983).

Christianity took an even sterner view of women and their sexuality. Paul was very much against what he described as the libertarian attitude to women in classical time: 'Women should keep quiet in the church, they must take a subordinate position . . . A man ought not to wear anything on his head for his is the image of God, while woman is only reflection of man's glory' (Paul I, Cor 11:3).

Islam has a lot in common with Christianity and Judaism, perhaps more with the latter. Like Judaism, the woman's sexual desire was acknowledged, and men were expected to fulfil their wife's sexual needs. Sexuality in general was not frowned upon and asceticism was not encouraged, although the notions of self-control, purification and self-punishment are all enshrined in the religious duty of fasting. Fasting is considered one of the five pillars of the Moslem faith, prescribed for one lunar month each year (Ramadan). Fasting is from dawn to sunset and entails both food and sexual abstinence. Menstruating women are considered religiously unfit for fasting. Independent from Ramadan, fasting for two days a week is also seen as desirable in many Islamic societies, in identification with the prophet's conduct in this respect.

Again in common with Judaism, women were raised to special position and esteem once they became mothers. The glorification of motherhood in Islam reached the point of almost sainthood, which is revealed in many of the prophet's sayings, for instance 'Heaven is under the feet of mothers' (El-Bokhary 1868). When Mohammed was asked whom should be regarded first, he answered 'mother' and when asked again he said 'mother' and yet again 'mother' for the third, and then 'father' (El-Bokhary 1868).

Islam also gives clear emphasis to man's lordship over woman: 'Men have authority over women because Allah has made the one superior to the other, and because they spend their wealth to maintain them' (Sura: Women, 4:34). One of the obvious reasons for the claim of man's superiority in this Qur'anic verse seems to derive from man's economic advantage. Women are expected to share in their husbands' wealth, and to be financially supported by them, but religion has also given women full economic independence which was endorsed by the Islamic law. Women are allowed the right to own and manage properties and dispose of their capital without their spouse's consent.

There is no better example of such economic power than that of Khadijah, Mohammed's first wife, who was a wealthy widow, twice married and traded on her own account. Mohammed was hired to work for her, as he was reputed for his honesty and integrity. She was the one who later proposed to him and married him despite being fifteen years his senior. She was his main source of support in spreading his message.

The consent of the woman to the marriage is a legal requirement in Islam. The marriage document is seen as a binding contract and in theory should allow the woman to put whatever conditions she wants prior to marriage.

However, there are still other aspects that are clearly seen as disadvantageous to women in Islam, such as the relative ease of divorce and indeed polygamy. The latter was regarded as an expression of the political and utilitarian understanding of marriage in Islam. Polygamy was seen as a solution to the problem that women in that period outnumbered men, who were systematically killed in battles. Polygamy was seen as a better fate for women than destitution or prostitution. There was also the need to populate this new Islamic nation in order to increase its power. This is the basis for the argument used by liberal Moslem scholars to outlaw polygamy as the social conditions that required it in the first place no longer exist.

A similar argument is being used with the issue of veiling, which came to be exclusively associated with Islam, although it is in fact much older than Islam. Veiling goes back to the Assyrians and is sanctioned by Hinduism and enshrined in both Judaism and Christianity. Its historical significance stems from the fact that it was considered at the time a status symbol. It distinguished free women from slaves. Islam found women of position veiled already and recommended veiling for the very same reason. Scholars argue that there has never in fact been an absolute religious requirement for it, and given the changes in social conditions there are no longer convincing grounds for keeping it (El-Ashmawi 1994, Darwish 1994).

Islam did not indeed prescribe any particular or exact style of veiling and the actual Qur'anic verse speaks more of modesty:

> Tell the believing women to lower their gaze and be modest and to display of their ornaments only that which is apparent, and to draw their veils over their bosoms and not to reveal their adornments, save to their husbands and fathers.
>
> (Sura: Light, 24:31)

Both men and women were expected to observe modesty in dress and conduct but the focus was clearly on women as the source of sexual seductiveness which poses a threat to social order. Interestingly, the word *Fetna* in the Arabic language means both woman's sexual seductiveness and social disruption. The concept of modesty changed over time and became perhaps more restrictive as society became more complicated. However, what was considered as 'appropriate veiling' remained variable as it was largely left open to individual interpretation. These days there is almost a continuum of veiling, ranging from the uniform black cloaks worn by the post-revolution Iranian women to the exclusive designer scarves worn by rich women in Egypt (Watson 1994). However, veiling in any shape or form is commonly perceived as a form of social control meant to segregate and render women invisible; this aspect of veiling is what normally concerns the liberal mind.

Nawal El-Saadawi, the outspoken Egyptian feminist, explained that the deterioration of women in Islam followed serious changes in society that continued to condemn women to more inferior positions, and which in her opinion had nothing or little to do with Islamic teaching. It became evident by the time of Harun al Rashid, a time of concentration of wealth in a clear patriarchy, that women were increasingly pushed to the background and were not expected to be seen except with their husbands or next of kin as decreed. It was the time that ushered in the Harem system which was to flourish later under the Turkish Ottoman empire (El-Saadawi 1980).

Arab women in the eyes of the West

The Arabs are historically the tribes which inhabited the Arab peninsula (currently Saudi Arabia). The mission of Mohammed (AD 632) is crucial in Arab history. A heterogeneous group of nations was assimilated to the Arabian Arabs through a process of Arabization and Islamicization. Some converted to Islam without adopting the Arabic tongue (Persians, Turks, Indians, Malysians, Indonesians) while others adopted the Arabic tongue without converting to Islam (Christians and Jews of Egypt, Lebanon, Syria and Morocco). The citizens of the following nations are collectively defined as Arabs by reason of the use of Arabic as their official, administrative and cultural language: Egypt, Syria, Jordan, Iraq, Lebanon, Sudan, Yemen, Libya, Tunisia, Algeria, Morocco, Saudi Arabia and other Gulf states. Recently, more nations joined the Arab league and regarded themselves as Arab, such as Mauritania, Djibouti and Eritrea.

Arab and Moslem became synonymous, and Islam started to be seen as the sole definer of the Arabic culture and subsequently of its women too. Condemned to live in the prison of harem, or hiding behind the veil, is the picture that the West has cultivated over the years of Moslem women and shaped accordingly its stereotypes.

Rana Kabbani, a Syrian woman writer, looked at how Europe mythologized the Middle East through its nineteenth-century travel literature and art. European nineteenth century paintings, particularly the French, celebrated the differences between eastern and western ideas of beauty and highlighted what the artists perceived as aesthetic contrasts; they narrated the East, said Kabbani, while painting it. The most famous is Ingre's *The Turkish Bath*, where the round shape of the painting imparts the rounded shape of its subjects, the rounded female, with rounded breasts, belly and thighs (Kabbani 1986).

Art conveyed the picture of the harem, a place, as Victor Hugo described, of

> hedonism where women generally nude, often voluptuous, unbridled with passion and full of eroticism . . . reclined the live-long day on a soft divan, adorned with gold, jewels and supporting upon a yielding pillow, those arms that indolence make so plump.
>
> (cited in Thornton 1985)

But the desirable woman in Orientalist paintings was hardly a foreign-looking woman; the subjects of the paintings were mostly fair-skinned Circassians. They had to look exotic without necessarily looking dark; the men, on the other hand, were the Negro slaves who guarded them with their swords (Kabbani 1986).

Lewis's famous painting, *The Harem*, depicts a man but in a classically stereotyped version of an Arab surrounded by his wives. Another subject was the depiction of the belly dancer, or the dancer of the East, which shocked the westerners who removed it from its local context and regarded it as a mysterious, provocative drama of the voluptuous body, in contrast to the ethereality of the ballerina of the West.

This theme was to continue in many of Matisse and Renoir's Odalisques; however, these two artists had a sympathetic eye towards their subject matter and appeared to have been exhilarated and enriched as artists by their experience of the Arab Moslem women they painted, who were mostly Algerian and Moroccan.

The other major determining source was literature, which did just the same in promoting these stereotypes. The main literary figures in this period were Burton, Flaubert and Lane. The most famous piece of literature was Burton's translation of *The Arabian Nights* (Burton 1954). It shaped the western fantasy of these obscure and exotic lands, where the male enjoyed absolute dominion and women only existed for his sexual pleasures. *The Arabian Nights* enjoyed the status, not only of a literary classic, but also of an ethnographic source (Meman 1995).

In *Manners and Customs of the Modern Egyptians*, Lane (1890) describes Egyptian women as: 'being the most licentious in their feelings . . . what liberty they have and most of them are not considered safe unless under lock and key, the most prudent of all husbands cannot guard against their intrigue'.

Some argued that this peculiar picture of Arab women was a kind of eccentric male depiction, determined to a great extent by the values of the authors and their own personal experiences. However, the women writers of this period were not in any way more candid; their impression was different but still equally negative, except perhaps for Lucie Duff-Gordon (1969), who was of the opinion that Egyptian husbands gave their womenfolk greater freedom than did British gentlemen.

Florence Nightingale depicted a negative picture after only a quarter of an hour's contact with Egyptian women:

> I felt like the Hypocrite in Dante's hell . . . and have never been so thankful for being a Christian woman; the quarter of an hour seemed to reveal to one what it is to be a woman in these countries . . . God save them, for it is a hopeless life.
>
> (Nightingale 1854)

The myth of the Harem has endured in the face of all political and cultural changes; there is a tendency to deny that any change in these countries has ever taken place or indeed was possible. The picture of the Harem to a greater or lesser extent is still regarded as a microcosm of the Middle East (Meman 1995).

This image was undoubtedly strengthened by the media coverage of post-revolution Iranian women, and the westerner's exposure to Gulf states through employment. The picture of women in Saudi Arabia came to be seen as representative of almost all Arab women in the region.

The Egyptian feminist movement

In the eighteenth century, Egypt had its first contact with European thought through the Napoleonic expedition. The French campaign introduced to Egypt printing and publishing. Journalism developed, and a wide translation movement began which made French thoughts, particularly those ideals of the French revolution, accessible to the Egyptians. The effect of this Napoleonic mission is strongly conveyed in Hugo's words: 'Prodigious, he stunned the land of prodigies . . . like a Mohammed of the Occident' (Hugo 1964).

By the nineteenth century, Khedive Ismael, a kind of Medici of Egypt, declared that Egypt was no longer in Africa and that Cairo was the Paris of the Orient. This was a period commonly referred to as the *belle époque*, epitomized by the building of the Cairo opera and the opening of the Suez Canal (Mostyn 1989). The most important economic change of this period was the integration of Egypt into a European economic system (Tucker 1986).

Major social changes happened in the political structure and particularly the legal system. Egypt secularized its law in the middle of the nineteenth century by adopting the French civil law, except for matters regulating marriage, divorce and inheritance –

the so called personal status laws – which continued to be governed by Islamic law with certain clauses for other religions. The education system also evolved into schools modelled on European lines, particularly French. The second Europeanizing force was obviously through the British presence in Egypt.

The Egyptian feminist movement began in the latter part of the nineteenth century, more or less around the same time as the Suffragettes in Britain and the feminists in France. It was ushered in with the publication of Qasim Amin's books *Tahrir-el-Mar'aa* (Women's Emancipation, 1899) and *El-Mar'aa El-gadida* (New Woman, 1901). The books declared the abolition of the veil and the social seclusion of women.

The entry of women into the realm of journalism was vital in strengthening the movement. Before the First World War, magazines in the Arabic language, such as *New Eve*, *The Egyptian Woman* and the *Daughter of the Nile*, appeared in Egypt dealing with the personal and social problems of Egyptian women. More feminist publications appeared in the inter-war period and these were mainly founded and edited by women (Lutfi El Said-Marsot 1977, 1978).

There was, however, one political magazine, not dedicated to women's issues, established by the actress Fatma El Youssef, called *Rose El Youssef*; it is still in circulation today and held in very high esteem by the Egyptian intelligentsia. Incidentally, Fatma El Youssef is the mother of the famous Egyptian writer Ihsan Abdel Kodous who came to be known as the Egyptian D. H. Lawrence, as he was the first to challenge some of the society's sexual taboos.

The ideological argument for the change in women's position was legitimated by the needs of the society and was to gain strength once the feminist movement entered the political arena. It was the 1919 anti-British demonstrations, led by the feminist Huda Shaarawi, at which women dropped the veil. This is reflected in one of the famous and outstanding Egyptian works of art, *The Egyptian Awakening*, by Mokhtar. The sculpture shows an Egyptian woman removing the veil, in juxtaposition to the sphinx, pointing to the desire to embrace her old history and reveal herself to the world again after years of hiding (Karnouk 1988).

Veiling, however, was never endorsed by the law in Egypt and was never adopted by the rural women of Egypt. At that time only the upper-class urban women did so. Lucie Duff-Gordon, an English woman who lived in Egypt in the 1860s, remarked that the Christians of Egypt were more fastidious than the Muslims in veiling (Duff-Gordon 1969). With the advent of the feminist movement, however, Egyptian urban women adopted European dress.

In 1923 Huda Shaarawi formed the league of women, which was responsible for passing resolutions regarding women's education, making elementary school education compulsory for all girls (Shaarawi 1986). Taha Hussain, a leading figure in the Egyptian cultural life of this century, fought for women's rights to higher education and risked his career as a university professor because of El-Azhar (the oldest and largest Islamic institution in the Middle East) opposition at the time. Taha Hussain won the battle, and the first entry of women students to Cairo University was in 1928.

The first generation of women graduates were highly influential in shaping women's consciousness and in promoting the feminist cause. At present, women constitute more than 30 per cent of the total number enrolled in the University every year. There are no recent accurate statistics to show exactly how many women are in employment now, but the figure among city dwellers is in the region of 60 per cent, and at least 20 per cent of these women hold a University degree. There is a respectable proportion of women who have doctorate degrees in their subjects, and many hold university professorial posts.

Laws were passed to protect women against discrimination on the basis of sex; they had equal right to education, to employment, to promotion and to equal pay. Women also gained other benefits such as paid, long maternity leave, which could be extended without jeopardizing their job security. Obligatory kindergartens were also provided (Sullivan 1987).

Women were accorded the right to vote in 1954, subsequent to a rather interesting sequence of events. The right to vote was granted after a number of feminist activists went on hunger strike. Nasser intervened, but he had first to make Sheikh El-Azhar, who was opposing the move, an ambassador to Yemen; soon after he was posted, the law was passed!

The Nasserite regime embraced the principles of socialism, endorsing the idea of a state-controlled economy; however, private ownership was not denied. The political regime was generally sympathetic to the woman's cause. Expansion of the government service programme took place, with a lot of expenditure targeted to education, cultural activities, health and guaranteed employment. The law gave women the right to parliamentary representation in the Egyptian People's Assembly, and thirty seats are reserved for this purpose, which led in due course to women succeeding in holding ministerial positions; three are currently in the cabinet.

This change in the position of women reflected itself in their clothes and appearance. Observers argued that by the early 1970s there was not a single veiled woman among the urban female population of Egypt. Women freely adopted the latest fashion, with revealing gowns and mini-skirts, which can be clearly seen in the actresses' dresses of the Egyptian movies at the time.

Not only did movies convey the liberated look, but the essence of this change was captured in progressive movies like *My wife is a general director*, which deals with the conflict of an architect who discovers that his wife was appointed the head of the company for whom he works. She earns in the end her husband's and other employees' respect and acceptance of her right to the post.

It is important to note that men's acceptance and the absence of hostility or overt discrimination to women in the workplace made it possible for women to see that work does not come into conflict with being a woman. Work and femininity at that time were to a great extent reconciled.

In Sadat's time the regime moved sharply to the right with the adoption of the open door policy. A new wealthy class emerged, *nouveau riche*, who benefited from the liberalization of the economy and the relaxation of rules. The emphasis was on display of wealth and consumerism. This was happening against a background of increasing economic difficulties for a lot of other people, resulting from unemployment, redundancies, or frozen state salaries against rising inflation. The regime feared that the socialist movement could gather momentum and sabotage the open door policy; hence, a new ideology strong enough to combat socialism was needed, and the only card to be played was the revival of Islam.

The new Islamic ideology mostly attracted those who felt disadvantaged by the system, although others also used religion as a tag to promote their commercial interests. In the process all values were reversed; ambivalence about the value of education started to emerge, as it became increasingly obvious that education was no longer a guarantor of work or a reasonable standard of living. Religiosity and piety became the new cherished values; these were enhanced by the increased exposure of Egyptians, through the exported labour force, to more strict and rigid Islamic societies like Saudi Arabia.

The move towards a free-market economy gradually changed the perception of society to women. The new enterprises saw women as a liability; their productivity was questioned, and the privileges conferred on them by law were condemned as costly. Women were subsequently seen as unfit for jobs, and adverts started to state clearly a preference for male applicants. The highest unemployment now in Egypt is among the most educated, especially among the technologically trained engineers. This theme was picked up again by the Egyptian cinema in a movie that bears the title *The resignation of a female nuclear scientist*, where the woman scientist is forced to resign her post as she can not employ a nanny for her child, the nanny's salary being much more than the salary she earns from the state-controlled research institute.

The Islamic ideology was used as a kind of reasoning for not employing women, with the notion being promoted that home is the right place for women. Work changed from a human right to a necessity; women only work if they have to, i.e. in cases of economic need. Women began to see themselves and their work devalued.

The ironic thing is that the pressure on women to achieve academically did not abate; they were still expected to do well in schools and universities, even if they are going to shelve their degrees afterwards. This neatly fits the description made by Selvini-Pallazoli (1985) of the modern woman: 'expected to put away their hard earned diplomas and wash the nappies'. Further, in reality and whether women wanted to work or not, most women had to work for economic reasons as most Egyptian families cannot survive at present on one salary.

With these changes, the feminist movement entered a new phase and began to be seriously challenged. Disillusionment, ideological vacuum, all gave way quickly to the new trend of Islamic fundamentalism which manifested itself in a return to the Islamic tradition in dress and behaviour. Women took up veiling in huge numbers and men grew beards. Analysts muttered that the Marxist beard has been replaced by the Islamic one. The social epidemic of veiling was resonant of Ionesco's famous play *Rhinoceros*, where he described people changing into rhinos at a very rapid rate; the metaphor was of course used at that time to indicate the rapid spread of communism (Ionesco 1962). Women who took up the veil were mostly young students, which meant that many of the young veiled women would have mothers or grandmothers who were still wearing the western dress. Many of these students came from the petty bourgeoisie, who had the opportunity to be educated to university level through free education, the legacy of the Nasserite phase, and who would otherwise have worked on a farm or a small factory (Hijab 1988).

There are certainly economic grounds for the return to the veil. In a survey conducted by the national centre for social studies in Egypt, 18 per cent resorted to Islamic dress for economic reasons, mainly to avoid competition in the latest fashion and the rising cost of the hairdressers. Twenty-five per cent regard it as fashionable; however, the majority paradoxically saw the veil as liberating, allowing women to move freely in the workplace by forcing society to see them more as human beings and less as sexual objects (Rugh 1987). MacLeod called it an 'accommodating protest', a peculiar way of resolving the conflicting struggle of the woman as wife/mother and the woman as worker. The contradictory intentions signalled by adopting the veil reflect the contradictory messages that face modern women today. This style of struggle involves both obedience and resistance (MacLeod 1991). The phenomenon of veiling, therefore, is not merely an unreflective continuation of tradition but more of a considered response on women's part to the way the world is changing (Baykan 1990).

The 'new veiling' phenomenon is seen as a global process and constitutes the subject of contemporary debate. The keenness of young Moslem women to take up the veil is also to be found in Europe. The veiling of Algerian girls in France, Pakistani in Britain and Turks in Germany is seen as a response to their feeling of confused cultural identity. Watson (1994) regarded the 'new veiling' as representing an act of resistance to forces of change, modernity and cross-cultural communication conditions – a deliberate act of choice that makes a personal statement in response to conflicting pressures and competing cultural values.

Other instances of Arab feminism

The feminist movement spread from Egypt to the rest of the Arab world. The first pan-Arab women's conference was convened by

Huda Shaarawi in Cairo in 1938. Shaarawi travelled to many Arab countries, encouraging women to set up unions; the General Federation of Arab Women was established in 1944. Women in Lebanon and Syria joined the Egyptian women in their struggle, and Lebanese women were in fact the first to be granted the right to vote in 1952. An Arab Women Solidarity Union was formed in 1985, headed by Nawal El-Saadawi.

With reference to personal status laws, Tunisia is considered the most advanced in the region. Muslim and Jewish courts were dissolved in 1957, and issues of personal status became civil matters. Revolutionary amendments to the laws were passed in connection to divorce, polygamy, marriage contract and the custody of children. Tunisia also has a national day for women.

Tunisia and Morocco are in the forefront of the Arab states in appointing women judges; this is significant since, under Qur'anic law, women are regarded as legal minors, and in courts two women are needed to witness to be equivalent to one man (Sura: The Cow, 2:282).

The women's question in Algeria did not progress sufficiently despite the role played by women in the Algerian struggle against the French, with legendary figures like Jamila Bouhrid (Hijab 1988). Algeria adopted socialism as a political system in the post-independence era, which again could explain the recent rise of Islamic ideology after the breakdown of the socialist structure.

Women of Turkey

The status of Turkish women is not dissimilar to that of Arab women. Historically, the position of women in Islam was perceived to be at its worst under the Turkish Ottoman rule. Most of the travellers' tales of the Orient, regardless of their distortions, were descriptive of either Egyptian or Turkish women (Meman 1995).

However, the status of women in Turkey changed dramatically under Attaturk's rule as Roberts explains in his book *The Triumph of the West*. In Turkey, Mustapha Kemal Attaturk played in the early part of this century a similar role to that sought by Khedive Ismail in Egypt in the latter part of the nineteenth century. He identified Turkey with the West and in 1925 officially adopted the western alphabet to replace the Arabic one for the new script. He also attacked the traditional dress and called his nation to adopt

European dress: 'A civilised international dress is worthy and appropriate for our nation' (cited in Roberts 1985).

The adoption of secularism was in response to the need to develop a national culture which was diametrically opposed to the Islamic multiculturalism of the Ottoman state (Stokes 1994). New legal and civic rights were given to women, like the right to education and to vote. Attaturk also declared the abolition of the veil. Turkish law, which was modelled on the Swiss civil code, only recognized civil marriages and banned polygamy, but as a result many children were being born who were legally illegitimate, and this later led the State to legitimize some eight million children (Hijab 1988). Turkey is divided now over its secular law and has similar problems with the rise of Islamic fundamentalism.

Women of the kibbutz

Kibbutz is a word that simply means a group in the Hebrew language. It is a utopian idea, commonly regarded as the most creative social experiment of this century (Leon 1969).

From the start the feminist component was significant in the formulation of the kibbutz ideology. The absence of the real family in the kibbutz was seen as symbolic of the revolt against the traditional patriarchal family structure. The objective of the kibbutz was to achieve true equality between the sexes through socializing all activities, including those that are seen as womanly activities such as household work.

Child rearing was traditionally handled in the kibbutz by the caretaker in the communal children house (*Mtapelet*), with minimal involvement on the part of the parents. This was supposed to free women to pursue other activities on equal terms with men.

However, in Golda Meir's biography, while she asserts that the kibbutz was one of the most successful frameworks for promotion of women's equality, she nonetheless remarked that women were normally given kitchen duties which made them feel that they were not on equal terms with men (Meir 1975).

In an extensive study of female kibbutzim over three generations, the authors were surprised to find that sex roles have not really changed despite the progressive structure of the kibbutz. They concluded that the kibbutz may have succeeded in realizing the ideals of making property and child care communal, remaining agricultural and reducing the importance of religion, but they failed to create the socio-sexual conditions they had hoped for (Tiger and Shepher 1977).

In keeping with this finding, recent changes in the structure of the kibbutz have indicated that women are increasingly taking more interest in caring and nurturing their children. This led to the emergence of something approaching a nuclear family structure within this communal setting. There are also other changes in women's perception of themselves, with more emphasis given to appearance and physical beauty, concepts that in the past were considered expressions of petty bourgeois decadence, not suitable for the socialist woman who was going to build society alongside the man (Kaffman and Sadeh 1989).

FROM CENTEOTL TO FRIDA KAHLO – THE CASE OF LATIN AMERICAN WOMEN

The power of the mother is central to Latin American mythology; in Peru it is Pachamama, the earth mother, and in Mexico it is Centeotl, the goddess of maize, the bringer of children. It is difficult, though, to talk about modern Latin Americans as a homogeneous entity; as a group they are composed of multiple ethnicities. Countries like Mexico and Peru were influenced by their earlier civilizations, and their conscience is shaped by the religion of the European invaders. Some experimented politically with communism or forms of socialism, and the impact of American policies on their life cannot be underestimated.

It could be that the only way to gain an insight into the situation of women in Latin America today is through women's art. In *Compañeras*, Duke tries to elucidate the changes that have happened to women in Latin America by analysing works of art by a number of women from Cuba, Brazil, Puerto Rico, Guatemala, Nicaragua and El Salvador, in which the artists express common and thoroughly modern concerns regarding sexuality, motherhood and gender (Duke 1985).

The most celebrated of all female artists is the Mexican Frida Kahlo, who became an international feminist icon. The Mexican writer Carlos Fuentes considers her a symbol of modern Mexico. Her surrealistic paintings, full of Aztec symbolism and influenced by communism, are seen as representing the condition of the modern woman today. Her famous picture, *The two Fridas*, where the two figures of herself are connected by a bleeding vein, is seen as not only symbolizing Frida's predicament of a dual Indian–European origin but also the split position that faces all modern women today (Kahlo 1995).

WOMEN IN POST-SOCIALIST EUROPE

The basic ethos of the socialist theory is egalitarianism, i.e. social equality regardless of class, race or gender. The liberation of women was seen as a vital ingredient in all socialist policies. Women's equal rights to education, employment and participation in political activity were all enshrined within the socialist system.

Critics of the system, however, saw that granting women working opportunities was not accompanied by socialization of housework and child-care tasks. These tasks remained the woman's responsibility on top of her work commitments, and in many instances they did not have the right to choose between employment and unemployment. As for her participation in political activity, this was controlled by the very fact that no political pluralism was allowed. Despite all the limitations of socialist policies, it is arguable whether the woman's cause is any better now under free-market ideology.

Russian feminists commented that the democratization of their society after Perestroika and Glasnost turned out to be a male project in which women were assigned the role of objects. In Mikhail Gorbachov's book, *Perestroika*, he lists the Soviet government's achievements on the woman's question and proposes a model for the future:

> We are proud of what the Soviet government has given women . . . women have been given every opportunity to receive an education, to have a career and to participate in social and political activities . . . but during our difficult and heroic history, we failed to pay attention to women's specific rights . . . women no longer have enough time to perform their everyday duties at home-housework, raising children and the creation of a good family atmosphere . . . we have begun to overcome this shortcoming . . . what we should do is to make it possible for women to return to their purely womanly mission.
>
> (cited in Posadskaya 1994)

Woman's best place is the home, became the message, not only in the old Soviet Union, but also in eastern Europe. The paternalistic emancipation of the old communist regime is disappearing and is gradually being replaced by the primacy of individual choice. Women increasingly find it difficult to work under the new economic climate, and their responsibilities toward the newly resettled family have increased (Posadskaya 1994).

Other developments affecting the role of women have included the rapid increase in pornography and prostitution in Hungary. Women are now liberally used as sexual objects, a development ironically going hand in hand with the rise in the practice of religion. There is in Poland the revival of Catholicism, which has been attributed to intellectual vacuums as well as the desire of some women to return to Christian values and spiritual aspects of life. The religious ideology clearly affirms the value of family life and Christian teaching: 'The Catholic women must not neglect their Christian responsibility, they must offer spiritual and religious guidance to their children, thereby asserting the church with the religious indoctrination in the Catholic faith' (cited in Yedlin 1978).

In one study which seeks to ascertain Polish women's reasons for working, the main reason was found to be the improvement of the family's financial position. Nearly one-third of the women were prepared to abandon full-time work in exchange for improved material gains. This was attributed to a rise in religious sentiment underlying these conservative views. Poland is a case of a society where religion is gradually filling the void that the death of communism has created. Catholicism is not only influencing women's rights to work and productivity but also their reproductive rights (Yedlin 1978).

In the Czech and Slovak republics women gained formal rights under the old regime; however, assimilation by the women of the communist ideology has been doubted. Communism is seen to have acted on women's behalf, and for some women today there is in reality no change except being economically worse off: 'What good in the new situation to me . . . I still get up early in the morning to be pushed around on the bus on my way to work. Now I do not even have enough money to put my washing in the laundry' (cited in Corin 1992).

There are features common to all countries, whether in Europe or elsewhere, that experimented with socialism and are now adopting a free-market policy. Under the socialist regime, there was full acceptance of women's work, and over-employment to insure full employment was the rule in these countries. With the economic reform, market forces are pushing the unproductive labour out, and women are more likely than men to be casualties of this exercise. It has been said that the dictatorship of the party has been replaced by the dictatorship of the market.

Under socialism, women were expected to be mothers, wives and professionals; however, this is subtly different from the super-woman concept I referred to earlier. The socialist precept did not necessarily see the wife and mother as separate from the professional; both are presented to women as complementary roles and not opposing or conflicting alternatives. It has been suspected therefore that gender role perception in a socialist society is different from that in a western democracy. To test this hypothesis, German and Bulgarian female students were compared. The German women prized what they considered as gender-specific qualities (empathy, tolerance, openness and friendliness), despite the fact that they recognized that society prizes, instead, assertiveness, competence and tenacity. The Bulgarians on the other hand prized qualities that are not normally connected with the female gender (forcefulness, ambition, courage, will power, initiative) and also recognized that these qualities are prized by society, so what they valued in themselves was not discrepant from what they saw as desired by society (Catina 1995).

So it seems that, in societies where socialist thinking prevailed for a time, the women internalized masculine qualities conducive to achievement without seeing this as discordant with their female gender. However, in capitalist democracies, women value in themselves qualities traditionally considered feminine and yet acknowledge that society praises quite different values. This creates a greater distance between their perception and the societal perception of their role.

BLACK FEMINISM

In her book *Ain't I a Woman*, bell hooks (1981) says:

No other group in America has so had their identity socialised out of existence as have black women. . . . We are rarely recognized as a group separate and distinct from black men, or as a

present part of the larger group 'women' in this culture . . .
When black people are talked about the focus tends to be on
black 'men' and when women are talked about the focus tends
to be on 'white' women.

This clearly highlights the dilemma that faces black women in a
white society where the issue of their gender identity cannot in
any way be separated from that of racism. It has been shown that
black women in the USA suffer two second-class citizenship positions, being black and being female, which is bound to cause
them considerable problems (Gray and Jones 1987).

Devaluation of black womanhood goes back to the sexual
exploitation of black women during slavery. Any racial integration
that took place in this century failed to include women. For
instance, while black men married white women in ever-increasing
numbers, white men did not marry black women. A complex
system of negative myths and stereotypes socialized white men to
regard black women as unsuitable marriage partners. The most
powerful of all is the stereotype that all black women were sexually
loose and morally inferior (hooks 1981).

Any positive images of black women, on the other hand, tended
to portray them as long-suffering, religious, self-sacrificing, maternal figures. Black women also played a role in emphasizing this
maternal look in order to shift the focus of attention away from
their sexuality, which led them to be labelled as 'matriarchs'.

The basis for this matriarchy myth is the fact that many black
women assume the role of mothers and providers. In so doing
they were seen to undermine man's power and constitute a threat
to the existing patriarchy. The term matriarch in reality does not
simply mean the 'mother provider', it means instead that women
have the right to exercise greater social and political power. This
certainly was not the case for black women who, by and large,
represent a socially and economically disadvantaged group (hooks
1981).

The sense of rejection felt by black women from the white community made them turn into themselves for approval and valuation
of their own worth. Black women's pride became increasingly
linked to an overall sense of black consciousness. This manifests in
the close relationship that black women have with other women,
which portrays a strong sense of comradeship: 'Stories written by
black women about black women abound in rich examples of the

dynamics of diversity in the same sex relationship among black women. Common to these writings is the theme of survival' (Mays 1985).

This is probably one of the reasons for the emergence of a black feminist movement independent from the white feminist movement in the USA. The white feminist movement was seen as reluctant to address the issue of racism and therefore betrayed the black feminist's aspirations toward achieving true equality.

THE OTHER WOMEN – THE ARGUMENT FOR IMMUNITY AND VULNERABILITY

From the above analysis of the position of women in non-western societies, it is now clear that most of them experience difficulties similar to those identified by feminist theorists in connection with eating pathology.

1 The majority of non-western societies have undergone social changes in the position of their women, with an increase in the number of educated and working women. Feminist movements, similar to those that arose in the West, also arose in some of these societies, and the traditional gender roles were questioned and revised. If the superwoman theory holds true in connection to eating pathology, all working women all over the world should in theory be in the same predicament.

2 It is true that the glorification of motherhood seems to be an undercurrent in most of the societies discussed, and it may be logical to expect women of these societies to welcome their mothering role. However the elevated position of the mother in these societies can also have its significant drawbacks, particularly on the perception of the woman as an individual. It is concomitant with the gigantic importance given to motherhood, that women are still viewed as reproductive machines. This puts enormous pressure on working women, who probably find it extremely difficult to delay having family early in their careers, although this is bound to have an enormous negative effect on their employment prospects and indeed their career progress (Nasser 1993).

As for the differentiation of daughters from their mothers, this process is also likely to be hindered. If anything, it could be more serious in these societies, as individuation from mother seems extremely difficult. These societies tend to see mothers as embodiments of all goodness and righteousness, epitome of sacrifices. Any attempt to criticize the mother's authority or rebel to establish one's own identity goes against the grain of the whole society, and can be expected to be met with disapproval.

3 The socio-economic changes that took place in non-western societies brought with them an expansion in education and increased emphasis on achievement. Achievement orientation has long been linked to the occurrence of eating pathology. Rapid economic changes were found to have the effect of widening the gap between social aspiration and social satisfaction, which is characteristic of developing economies. The frustrated need for achievement generates a deprived or oppressed group who exert pressure for social change in their struggle to fulfil their achievement aspirations and subsequently come into conflict with the prevailing political system (Feierabed et al. 1973). This seems to apply to the recent emergence of extreme Islamicist groups, who give expression, through political dissidence and an alternative ideology, to the frustrations and uncertainties arising from a sense of cultural disruption felt in these societies.

For women, revival of religion was seen as a way of responding to conflicting cultural messages that expect them to fulfil contradictory roles. The 'new veiling' phenomenon was described as an act of rebellion and obedience at the same time – a social analysis similar to that made of the anorexic position.

Revival of religion has in fact been studied in connection to eating pathology, where it has been said that the Christian vigil against sin was also a vigil against fat (Schwartz 1986). Among anorexics, girls who placed high importance on their religion were thinner than those who placed low importance, and the thinnest ever was one who professed strengthening of religion (Joughin et al. 1991).

A clear relationship was also found between the revival of fundamentalist Christian belief in the USA and dieting. There were more reports of anorexia nervosa among daughters of the families of fundamentalist Christians. This was explained on the basis that too much emphasis was placed on externals and appearance, with rigidity of thinking particularly with reference to moral issues and gender ideology (Gordon 1990).

So it seems that there is no convincing basis to continue with the assumed immunity theory of the *other* women. It is clear that the pressures that are hypothesized to increase western women's propensity to eating disorders are shared by all other women. Does that mean that the disease of western women will indeed become a global phenomenon? Possibly yes; however, the issue is not whether women are expected to be superwomen or whether their anorexia is a form of hunger strike against the tyranny of patriarchy. It is perhaps more to do with the degree to which women's expectations of themselves are reconciled with those of their society. It is the degree of concordance between society's and individual's values that is, in my opinion, important here. In societies, for instance, where the work of women was taken for granted, and where their sense of value appeared to derive from taking part in an overall social philosophy, there was no correlation between sense of inner worth and external appearance.

Now, in the absence of any clear political or social framework, there is a confusion as to what is really expected of women. The higher the degree of societal ambivalence about its own expectations of women, the greater the ambiguity that women experience of their own role. This sense of confusion is to a large extent related to the recent changes in the economic system worldwide, particularly after the death of communism. Women are most likely to be easy casualties of the new market forces for all the reasons I have already mentioned.

If eating disorders are indeed metaphors, as has been suggested, it is likely that what they symbolize now encompasses this social disruption and cultural confusion. So perhaps eating pathology is not after all about 'to be or not to be a woman', it is simply about 'to be or not to be' in the face of the increasing complexities of life.

Chapter 5

Culture: between differences and commonalities

Culture is one of the most elusive terms in the history of modern thought. In anthropology it refers to social heritage and encompasses ideas, beliefs, aesthetic perceptions and values. The term culture has been in common usage for nearly a century and yet there has not been any agreement on its definition or an understanding of its interaction with variables like race, nationality, social class, literacy or religion.

There may be no operational definition of culture, but the trend in the study of culture and psychopathology has been to divide the world into western and non-western cultures. The West, as I mentioned before, corresponded to what is European or North American, while the non-West became synonymous with the rest of the world. The issue of time was clearly neglected, and the common view was that non-western cultures were traditional, static and remote from the modernization process that was going on in the western world.

The interface between culture and civilization was readily acknowledged in regard to western culture, with Europeanism assumed to have its roots in the Greek civilization. In the case of non-western cultures, on the other hand, a clear distance has always been maintained between them and their respective past civilizations. This is perhaps particularly evident in the case of Egypt, with modern Egypt appearing to be far removed from its ancient past.

This is not to mention the contribution of Egyptian civilization to Greek thought in the first place. Bernal (1987) argues in his book *Black Athena* that the trend towards disconnecting Egypt from Classical Greece and diminishing its influence on Greek thought began in the eighteenth century with the rise of Romanticism and racism which were the two major forces prevailing at that time in both Britain and Germany. The Romantics saw Greece not only as the epitome of Europe but also its pure childhood. The Greek civilization in their view could not have been the result of the mixture of native Europeans and colonizing Africans and Semites.

The relationship between knowledge and experience that is culturally transmitted and that which derives from individual development is not yet fully understood. Ethnicity is often confused with race and nationality; when it is used as synonymous with race it sustains notions of genetic transmission of beliefs and assumes a correlation between the colour of the skin and different value systems. Fernando (1988) points to the fact that race, culture and ethnicity are interrelated in complex ways depending on historical and social forces. However, race and ethnicity are the criteria now commonly applied to infer social characteristics, while culture is disregarded. In multiracial, multicultural societies, the concept of ethnicity is identified through various social, political and economic pressures. The most significant of these pressures is racism, which tends to group people according to their perceived racial similarity. This problem is clearly highlighted in attempts to define the ethnicity of the immigrant population and their offspring, where it implies an inheritance of the family ethnicity regardless of the influences of the host society or indeed the immigrants' perception of their own true ethnic identity.

The roles of language and religion in defining cultures are constantly being debated. Some argue that culture is mainly determined by a shared language. However, there are groups, for example in Europe, that share similar values and beliefs without sharing a common language.

In contrast, others regard religion as a major denominator of cultural definitions. If religion is to be accepted as the main denominator, there are risks in assuming uniformity, only by reasons of subscribing to one religion, of groups that are historically and socially diverse. This is commonly the case with Islamic cultures, where their historical diversity is constantly ignored and all Islamic nations are considered culturally uniform by virtue of their religion. If the argument for the centrality of religion is to be pursued, European Christians should also in theory share the same cultural heritage as Africans who also happened to be Christian. If it is then argued that Christian Africans have been christianized by European forces, this would also appear to be the case in many Islamic nations that have been Islamicized by similar processes.

The contribution of Islam to the making of cultures is not only limited to the Middle or the Far East, it has even contributed to the cultural definition of many European states. Apart from the well-known example of Spain, Islamicization did also take place in Crete and Sicily; the names of the streets in Sicily were in Arabic until Mussolini's time. The Turkish Islamic rule of the Austro-Hungarian empire is yet another example.

The theological definition of human groupings, where nationality becomes synonymous with one's religion, is a political phenomenon that started in this century with the advent of Zionism. Now Islamicism is gradually acquiring more or less the same political status as Zionism. The differentiation of people on the basis of religion is extremely important now, particularly in view of what is happening in Bosnia. One wonders why the Moslems of the former European Yugoslavia are now emerging as a distinct cultural group.

On what basis then do we make cultural definitions, if both language and religion are unsatisfactory criteria?

Economics obviously plays an important role in this argument, as will be shown later. And yet equating the cultural make-up of nations with their economic standing is rather confusing and simplistic. Applying the concept of 'third worldness' to particular cultures only refers to the degree of their economic development. It also creates problems regarding the definition of wealthy countries that are only developed in terms of resources – for example, oil-rich countries.

However, if the issue of wealth is considered indirectly related to the level of industrialization and technological progress, there still remains a major problem concerning some nations that are wealthy and technologically advanced but are still clearly non-western – Japan, for example, and indeed many other countries of the Far East that are rapidly following Japan's example.

Despite the intrinsic heterogeneity of culture, and the complexities that this concept embodies, it is my contention that we are all now moving towards a globally unified culture. This is not by any means a new idea; the globalization process was set in motion through modern imperialism. Goethe predicted in the early part of the nineteenth century that the Orient and the Occident 'can no more be severed'. However, his view was later challenged by Kipling, who insisted that East was East and West was West (Hourani 1991).

In his book *Culture and Imperialism*, Said (1994) affirms the importance of understanding the evolution of this globalization process and how the colonial past has paved the way to it:

> To ignore or otherwise discount the overlapping experience of westerners and non-westerners, the interdependence of cultural terrain in which coloniser and colonised coexisted . . . is to miss what is essential about the world in the past century.

Many of the children of the so-called non-western cultures grew up to read western works of literature. For instance, Shakespeare, Ibsen, Brecht, Sartre, Beckett were all translated into Arabic and performed on the Egyptian stage. This is likely to have been the case in many other countries too. Said quotes L. R. James who said that Beethoven belongs as much to West Indians as he does to Germans, since his music is now part of the human heritage. Said continues to question the assumption that there are books for every nation, locally produced books that are assertive of one's own cultural identity. Any local culture could not in any case have been that pure (even if there is such a thing as pure culture), since many of those who shaped local cultures have been exposed to these westernizing forces. Major cultural figures in the non-West like Taha Hussain, who is considered to be the most important architect of modern Egyptian culture, viewed Europeanism as at the roots of that culture. He and similar cultural figures are often regarded as an elite group, but Taha Hussain was elite only in his intellect. He himself was a poor villager who lost his eyesight through his family's ignorance, and despite his poverty and blindness made it to the Sorbonne.

The identification with Europe in the past appeared to be more of a westernization of intellect. The Europeanization process that started in the nineteenth century has largely been replaced by Americanization in the latter part of this century. The new process is perhaps more concerned with the westernization of the market, i.e. the selling of a look, image, appearance. The world today is becoming more globalized because it is becoming more standardized.

This has certainly been facilitated by the deregulated media, with their emphasis on a certain look. The media now seem to play a major role in shaping this new universal culture. Mass media are purchasable commodities and, by and large, affordable. Mass media also confine themselves to simple imagery and clear messages that are easy to imitate and too powerful to ignore. Media have become globally accessible and resist and defy any attempts at regulation. It is doubtful if there remains a media-free culture in the age of television, videos and satellite broadcast. Information technology is also playing a similar role, with people all over the world now easily communicating with each other on the Internet (Nasser 1994).

The whole world now, including areas that were once considered far outposts of the western world, is rapidly integrating into this global 'superculture' (Weiss 1994). What every youth anywhere in the world now wants or aspires to, are the blue jeans, the designer T-shirt, the Big Mac and the Michael Jackson albums.

The impact of American culture is not in fact only limited to non-western societies with developing economies; if anything it is increasingly affecting policies in the whole of Europe. In his book *The State We're In* Hutton (1995) comments on the deregulation of the economy and its influence on deregulating the system of values in Britain today. These changes, as he says, have affected the deepest parts of the British psyche.

Market economies are based on the notion that the economic world is an extension of the natural world, governed by its natural laws. Human conduct is reduced to a ranking of economic choices in which costs and benefits are accurately and consistently weighed up one against another. Markets are not value-free economic structures; humanity is redefined as customers who consume products. The marketization of society, as Hutton says, may be an abstract concept, but its impact on everyday life is real enough: 'Market forces takes a terrible toll of the social groupings that represent humanity, from parenting our children to the reliability of public transport'. The inequality the system breeds is not about income, but it is about the loss of predictability and security of income.

Market strategies, to work properly, need strong social institutions; however, the opposite has taken place. The welfare state has been attacked as fostering dependency, besides being seen by the short-termist as economically non-viable. The primacy of individual choice that is now being promoted by market philosophy celebrates the private domain and leads to increasing social isolation of the individual. Hence, market forces ought to be seen as contributing to the breakdown of the culture of commitment to organization and undermining the individual's sense of belonging to a collective social structure.

Although Britain has been in the vanguard of the market experiment, it is certainly not alone. Since 1979 there has been a worldwide growth in the belief that markets are the solution to all economic difficulties, and the economic system has been taken up by a great majority of societies (Hutton 1995).

The effect of this economic transformation on culture is beginning to be seen in eastern Europe after the decline of communism and has also been witnessed in other societies which underwent a socialist experience. The disappearance of the social provisions that were part of the socialist regime is currently being blamed for the increasing sense of social fragmentation and the inequalities that are now deeply felt by the people of these nations.

The destruction of social networks is obviously bound to affect women more, since they were largely protected in their education, health, employment and child care rights under socialist policies. Capitalist societies, on the other hand, have always been ambivalent about the position of women in the workplace and were very slow to make provisions to help women to work. This certainly explains part of the dilemma that faced many women in these societies and which, instead of being blamed on the lack of provision for women's needs within the economic structure, was more vaguely attributed to these women's 'western status'.

With the worldwide adoption of free markets, nowhere in the world can women feel secure about their rights, particularly their work rights, and especially those related to child care. Under profit-motivated economies, these kind of provisions will be greatly undermined as they are commonly viewed as not cost-effective.

Cost-effectiveness and increased efficiency are the pillars of market philosophy, which means that any surplus in the labour force has to go. To compete in the labour market, women will either have to deny their own biology or end up staying at home. Traditional views promoting women's duty to return home have been revived to serve the new economic structure. These changes, as I said, are most likely to be acutely felt in the societies where women enjoyed to a great extent an acceptance of their work rights and there was greater evidence of state commitment towards adequate provisions to make working possible for women. This situation will understandably lead to further confusion about gender roles.

Inherent in the market economy is the issue of standardization. The drive to standardization is enhanced by the need for increased efficiency. In order to achieve this goal, any differences, eccentricities and excesses have to be cut out of the system and humanity has to be streamlined. Ironically, the same system talks of the rights of the individual and promotes the notion of free choices. The unlimited options that are presented to the individual are also accompanied by a restriction of power to exercise them. In reality the individual is an individual only when it comes to fighting his own corner and finding a niche for himself in the world. Competitiveness is the rule; those who possess it will remain in the system, and those who do not will be out.

Those who consistently fail to be part of the system will eventually adopt an extremist position. Their extremism represents their resentment at being unable to fit into society. The more the drive towards standardization, the more will be the tendency to behave in an extreme manner, which could finally lead to the development of 'subcultures of extremism' within the framework of the 'global and standardized superculture'.

The rise in fanaticism in many areas of our life today, manifesting in religious extremism and terrorism, is a phenomenon that requires urgent understanding within the framework of this hypothesis. There is no doubt that the altered value system that accompanied the new market philosophy was associated with a strong need to fill the ideological vacuums that resulted from the death of communism and the decline of the paternalistic structure of the old capitalism. The rise in fundamentalist religious ideology could also be seen as politically serving the new economic structure and as important to its survival. However, these forms of fanaticism are viewed by those who adopt them as a search for a sense of belonging, a rebellious stance arising from their feeling excluded by the system, a distorted act of heroism or indeed a quest for re-definition against this perceived cultural globalization. The ultimate result, however, is increased cultural disruption and fragmentation.

Fanaticism is clearly an act of overt rebellion that can still be seen as 'rebellion by conformity' through blind adherence to an alternative ideology. The notion of rebellion through conformity has been raised in connection with anorexia nervosa, where the woman is said to be trying to deny her womanhood by becoming extremely thin but by doing so she is also conforming to the thinness ideal.

In the second chapter of this book I pointed to the fact that, over the course of time, neurosis took different shapes and forms in response to changing cultural situations. This was clearly seen in the case of hysteria and anorexia nervosa; the argument is that both conditions do in fact make a statement in reaction to certain social conditions, since freedom and repression of both sexuality and appetite have always been common human concerns throughout history.

The issue of food consumption and food control has indeed preoccupied humanity particularly at times when cultures appeared to be at a crossroads. Civilization was said to corrupt appetite, which could result in gluttony. This explains why all civilizations appeared to have 'vomited' at some stage in their development, arguably at their peak!

Individuals will undoubtedly continue to swing on the pendulum of chaos and control, be it in the area of food or indeed in any other areas of their life. The spectrum of morbidity will possibly include obesity, anorexia and bulimia, hysteria and teenage pregnancies. It could be argued that it should include any other extremist behaviours that are also clearly shown to be caused by the same underlying sociocultural dynamics.

Some will understandably find it difficult to accept the pathologization of teenage pregnancies or fanatic religious behaviour in the same way as recognized neurosis. However, they are all located on the same spectrum of social morbidity that in my opinion only takes different forms or guises but is still deeply rooted in the cultural structure.

I could be blamed for reading too much into the symbolism of eating disorders or indeed the whole concept of neurosis, and yet one cannot really afford to ignore or underestimate the role of culture in all of this. Now the changes within culture have a global perspective, which means that these conditions could become universally prevalent. Human distress is currently being shaped by more or less the same forces. We will certainly be ill-advised if we continue to believe that there are isolated pockets of humanity that are remote from these forces. Even if there are still such groups, it is debatable that we would be better informed about the cultural interactions with psychopathology if we studied them.

If we carry on with these old notions we will be concerned with concepts that are outdated and bear little or no resemblance to what is truly happening in the real world. There are now common preoccupations, concerns, frustrations and aspirations as well as standard appearances prescribed to humanity at large.

We will also be equally wrong if we misconstrue any extremist religious or nationalistic groups as representing any mainstream culture. However, we certainly need to seriously examine these phenomena, not because they define culture, but because they are byproducts of it.

Eating disorders are extreme forms of behaviour that are symptomatic of an underlying human distress. The distress is caused by the loss of the relation of the self to the other, and the loss of one's ability to understand the prevailing system and be part of it. This distress is reactive to the sense of confusion, disorganization and disharmony felt by many who need to be on the inside of the system and yet are always outside it. It is true that these disorders occur predominantly in women, but the reason does not lie in being a woman, it is more to do with the fact that women, for many obvious reasons, have been vulnerable to the effects of these cultural changes. There is nonetheless an indication that men are increasingly becoming affected by these conditions. Taking into account all the arguments I have advanced above, I am led to the conclusion that cultural forces are responsible for this modern morbid phenomenon. It is a response to an ambiguous double-bind culture that is felt to be both orderly and chaotic, coherent and fragmented, standardized and individualistic. Palmer (1979) suggested that bulimia could be redefined as a dietary chaos syndrome. These disorders, as we know very well now, are not really about weight or eating and if we accept that they are expressions of culture, would it not be more appropriate to call them *culture chaos syndromes*?

This question is not meant to convey a gloomy picture of the culture we live in or confuse the issue of eating pathology with other issues that some may consider to be totally unrelated. My main aim is to stimulate debate on the role of culture in causing these particular disorders and show that we can no longer continue to pretend to be interested in the issue of the relationship between these disorders and culture without seeking to achieve a proper and deeper understanding of what we really mean by that concept called 'culture'.

Bibliography

1 THE SOCIOCULTURAL MODEL OF EATING PATHOLOGY

American Psychiatric Association (1993) *Diagnostic and Statistical Manual of Mental Disorders*, Washington DC, fourth edition.

Anderson, A. and Di Domenico, L. (1992) Diet vs shape content of popular male and females magazines: A dose response relationship to the incidence of eating disorders?, *Int. J. Eating Disord.* **11**: 283–287.

Azuma, Y. and Henmi, M. (1982) A study on the incidence of anorexia nervosa in schoolgirls, *Annual Report of the Research Group into Eating Disorders, Japan*, pp. 30–34.

Bennett, W. and Gurin, J. (1982) *The Dieter's Dilemma: Eating Less and Weighing More*, New York: Basic Books.

Bray, G. A. (1976) *The Obese Patient*, Philadelphia: Saunders.

Bruch, H. (1973) *Eating Disorders and Obesity: Anorexia and the Person Within*, New York: Basic Books.

—— (1978) *The Golden Cage: The Enigma of Anorexia Nervosa*, London: Open Books.

Brumberg, J. (1988) *Fasting Girls: The Emergence of Anorexia Nervosa as a Modern Disease*, Cambridge, Mass.: Harvard University Press.

Bunnell, D., Shenker, R., Nussbaum, M., Jacobson, M. and Cooper, P. (1990) Subclinical versus formal eating disorder: differentiating psychological features, *Int. J. Eating Disord.* **9**: 357–362.

Button, E. J. and Whitehouse, A. (1981) Subclinical anorexia nervosa, *Psychol. Med.* **11**: 509–516.

Canning, H. and Meyer, G. (1966) Obesity – its possible effects on college acceptance, *New England J. Med.* **275**: 1172–1174.

Cash, T. E. and Janda, I. H. (1984) The eye of the beholder, *Psychology Today* December: 46–52.

Chiodo, J. and Latimer, P. (1983) Vomiting as a learned weight control technique in bulimia, *J. Behav. Ther. Exp. Psychiat.* **14** (2): 131–135.

Clark, K. (1980) *Feminine Beauty*, London: Weidenfeld & Nicolson.

Clarke, M. and Palmer, R. L. (1983) Eating attitudes and neurotic symptoms in university students, *Br. J. Psychiat.* **142**: 299–304.

Cooper, P. G. and Fairburn, C. G. (1982) Self-induced vomiting and bulimia nervosa: an undetected problem, *Br. Med. J.* **284**: 1153–1155.

—— (1983) Binge eating and self-induced vomiting in the community: a preliminary study, *Br. J. Psychiat.* **142:** 139–144.

—— (1984) Binge eating and self-induced vomiting and laxative abuse: a community study, *Psychol. Med.* **14:** 401–410.

Crisp, A. H. (1970) Pre-morbid factors in adult disorders of weight, with particular reference to primary anorexia nervosa (weight phobia): a literature review, *J. Psychosomatic Res.* **14:** 1–22.

Dally, P. (1989) *Elizabeth Barrett Browning: A Psychological Portrait*, London: Macmillan.

Dancyger, I. and Garfinkel, P. (1995) The relationship of partial syndrome of eating disorders to anorexia nervosa and bulimia nervosa, *Psychol. Med.* **25:** 1018–1025.

Druss, R. and Silverman, J. (1979) Body image and perfectionism of ballerinas: comparison and contrast with anorexia nervosa, *Gen. Hosp. Psychiat.* 115–121.

Duddle, M. (1973) An increase of anorexia nervosa in a university population, *Br. J. Psychiat.* **123:** 711–712.

Dwyer, J., Feldman, J., Seltzer, C. and Mayer, J. (1969) Body image in adolescents: attitudes toward weight and perception of appearance, *Am. J. Clin. Nutrition* 30: 1045–1056.

Fallon, A. and Rozin, P. (1985) Sex differences in perceptions of desirable body shape, *J. Abnorm. Psychol.* **94** (1): 102–105.

Frank, K. (1990) *Emily Bronte: A Chainless Soul*, London: Hamish Hamilton.

Garfinkel, P., Lin, B., Goering, P., Spegg, C., Goldbloom, D., Kennedy, S., Kaplan, A. and Woodside, B. (1995) Bulimia nervosa in a Canadian sample: prevalence, co-morbidity, early experience and psychosocial functioning, *Am. J. Psychiat.* **152:** 1052–1058.

Garfinkel, P. E., Moldofsky, H. and Garner, D. M. (1980) The heterogeneity of anorexia nervosa: bulimia as a distinct sub-group, *Arch. Gen. Psychiat.* **37:** 1036–1040.

Garfinkel, P., Goldbloom, D., Garner, D., Davis, R., Olmsted, M. and Halmi, K. (1992) Body dissatisfaction in bulimia nervosa: relationship to weight and shape concerns and psychological functioning, *Int. J. Eating Disord.* **11:** 151–161.

Garner, D. M. and Garfinkel, P. E. (1979) The Eating Attitude Test: an index of the symptoms of anorexia nervosa, *Psychol. Med.* **9:** 273–279.

—— (1980) Sociocultural factors in the development of anorexia nervosa, *Psychol. Med.* **10:** 483–491.

Garner, D. M., Garfinkel, P. E., Schwartz, D. and Thompson, M. (1980) Cultural expectations of thinness in women, *Psychiat. Rep.* **47:** 483–491.

Garner, D., Olmsted, M. and Garfinkel, P. (1983) Does anorexia nervosa occur on a continuum? *Int. J. Eating Disord.* **2** (4): 11–20.

Goldblatt, P. B., Moore, M. E. and Stunkard, A. J. (1965) Social factors in obesity, *J. Am. Med. Assoc.* **192:** 97–102.

Gordon, R. (1990) *Anorexia and Bulimia: Anatomy of a Social Epidemic*, Cambridge, Mass.: Basil Blackwell.

Gull, W. W. (1868) The Address in Medicine delivered before the Annual Meeting of the BMA at Oxford, *Lancet* **2:** 171.

Halmi, K. A., Falk, R. F. and Shwartz, E. (1981) Binge eating and vomiting: a survey of a college population, *Psychol. Med.* **11**: 697–706.

Healy, K., Conory, R. M. and Walsh, N. (1985) The prevalence of binge eating and bulimia in 1,063 college students, *J. Psychiat. Res.* **19**: 161–166.

Herzog, D., Norman, D., Rigotti, N. and Pepose, M. (1986) Frequency of bulimic behaviours and associated social maladjustment in female graduate students, *J. Psychiat. Res.* **20** (4): 355–361.

Hoek, H. (1993) Review of the epidemiological studies of eating disorders, *Int. Rev. Psychiat.* **5**: 61–74.

Hoek, H., Bartelds, A., Bosveld, J., van der Graaf, Y., Limpens, V., Maiwald, M. and Spaaij, M. (1995) Impact of urbanisation on detection rates of eating disorders, *Am. J. Psychiat.* **152** (9): 1272–1285.

Howat, P. and Saxton, A. (1988) The incidence of bulimic behaviour in a secondary school and university population, *J. Youth and Adolesc.* **17** (3): 221–231.

Imm, P. and Pruitt, J. (1991) Body shape satisfaction in female exercisers and non-exercisers, *Women's Health* **17** (4): 87–96.

International Classification of Mental and Behavioural Disorders (ICD 10), Clinical description and diagnostic guidelines (1992) Geneva: WHO.

Johnson-Sabine, E., Wood, K., Patton, G., Mann, A. and Wakeling, A. (1988) Abnormal eating attitudes in London school girls: A prospective epidemiological study: factors associated with abnormal response on screening questionnaires, *Psychol. Med.* **18**: 615–622.

Jones, D. J., Fox, M. M., Babigan, H. M. and Hutton, H. E. (1980) Epidemiology of anorexia nervosa in Monroe County, New York: 1960–1976, *Psychosomatic Med.* **42**: 551–558.

Katzman, M. A., Wolchik, S. A. and Brauer, S. L. (1984) The prevalence of frequent binge eating and bulimia in a non clinical college sample, *Int. J. Eating Disord.* **3**: 53–61.

Kendell, R. E., Hall, D. G., Hailey, A. and Babigan, H. M. (1973) The epidemiology of anorexia nervosa, *Psychol. Med.* **3**: 200–203.

Killen, J., Taylor, B., Telch, M., Sylor, K., Maron, D. and Robinson, T. (1985) Self induced vomiting and laxative and diuretic use among teenagers: precursors of the binge purge syndrome, *J. Am. Med. Assoc.* **255**: 144–147.

King, M. B. (1986) Eating disorders in General Practice, *Br. Med. J.* **293**: 1412–1414.

—— (1989) Eating disorders in General Practice population: prevalence, characteristics and follow-up at 12–18 months, *Psychol. Med.* Monograph Suppl. **14**: 134.

King, M. and Mezey, G. (1987) Eating behaviour of male racing jockeys, *Psychol. Med.* **17**: 249–253.

Larkin, G. C. and Pines, H. E. (1979) No fat persons need apply – experimental studies of the overweight stereotype and hiring preference, *Sociol. Work and Occupations* **6**: 312–327.

Lasègue, C. (1873) De l'anorexie hystérique, *Arch. Gen. de Med.* 385. Reprinted in R. M. Kaufman and M. Heinman (eds) (1964) *Evolution of Psychosomatic Concepts: Anorexia Nervosa, a Paradigm*, New York: International University Press.

Lawrence, M. (1984) *The Anorexic Experience*, London: The Women's Press.

Lucas, A., Beard, C., O'Fallon, W., Kurland, L. (1991) 50-year trends in the incidence of anorexia nervosa in Rochester, Minnesota: a population based study, *Am. J. Psychiat.* **148**: 917–922.

Mann, A. H., Wakeling, A., Wood, K., Monck, E., Dobbs, R. and Szmukler, G. (1983) Screening for abnormal eating attitudes and psychiatric morbidity in an unselected population of 15 year old school girls, *Psychol. Med.* **13**: 573–580.

Mann, G. V. (1975) The influence of obesity on health, *New England J. Med.* **291**: 178–185.

Meadows, G. N., Palmer, L. L. and Newball, E. U. M. (1986) Eating attitudes and disorders in young women: a general practice based study, *Psychol. Med.* **16**: 351–357.

Mitchell, J., Pyle, R. and Eckert, E. (1991) Diet pill usage in patients with bulimia nervosa, *Int. J. Eating Disord.* **10** (2): 233–237.

Morgan, H. and Russell, G. F. M. (1975) Value of family background and clinical features as predictors of long term outcome in anorexia nervosa: 4 year follow up study of 41 patients, *Psychol. Med.* **5**: 355–371.

Moses, N., Banilivy, M. and Lifshitz, F. (1989) Fear of obesity among adolescent girls, *J. Paed.* **83** (3): 393–398.

Nylander, I. (1971) The feeling of being fat and dieting in a school population, *Acta Sociol. Med. Scand.* **I**: 17–26.

Ohezeki, T., Hanaki, K., Motozumi, H., Ishitani, N., Matsuda-Ontahara, H., Suunaguchi, M., and Shiraki, K. (1990) Prevalence of obesity, leanness and anorexia nervosa in Japanese boys and girls aged 12–14 years, *Ann. Nutrition and Metabolism* **34**: 208–212.

Orbach, S. (1986) *Hunger Strike: The Anorectic's Struggle as a Metaphor for our Age*, New York: Norton.

Palmer, R. L. (1979) The dietary chaos syndrome: a useful new term? *Br. J. Med. Psychol.* **52**: 187–190.

—— (1993) Weight concern should not be a necessary criterion for the eating disorders: a polemic, *Int. J. Eating Disord.* **14** (4): 459–465.

Patton, G. (1988) The spectrum of eating disorder in adolescence, *J. Psychosomatic Res.* **32** (6): 579–584.

Polivy, J., Zeitlin, S., Herman, P. and Baal, A. (1994) Food restriction and binge eating: a study of former prisoners of war, *J. Abnorm. Psychol.* **103**: 409–411.

Pyle, R. L., Mitchell, J. E., and Eckert, E. E. (1983) The incidence of bulimia in freshman college students, *Int. J. Eating Disord.* **2**: 75–85.

Rand, C. and Kuldau, J. M. (1991) Restrained eating (weight concerns) in the general population and among students, *Int. J. Eating Disord.* **10**: 699–708.

Rathner, G. and Messner, K. (1993) Detection of eating disorders in a small rural town: an epidemiological study, *Psychol. Med.* **23**: 175–184.

Richert, A. J. and Hummers, J. A. (1986) Patterns of physical activity in college students at possible risk of eating disorders, *Int. J. Eating Disord.* **5** (4): 757–763.

Rubinstein, H. (1930) *The Art of Feminine Beauty.* New York: Liveright.

Russell, G. F. M. (1970) Anorexia nervosa: its identity as an illness and its treatment. In J. Harding-Price (ed.) *Modern Psychological Medicine,* vol. II, pp. 131–164, London: Butterworths.

—— (1977) The present status of anorexia nervosa (Editorial), *Psychol. Med.* **7**: 363–367.

—— (1979) Bulimia nervosa: an ominous variant of anorexia nervosa, *Psychol. Med.* **9**: 429–448.

—— (1985) The changing nature of anorexia nervosa, *J. Psychiat. Res.* **19** (2/3): 101–109.

Schwartz, D. M., Thompson, M. G. and Johnson, C. L. (1986) Anorexia nervosa and bulimia: the socio-cultural context, *Int. J. Eating Disord.* **1**: 20–36.

Schwartz, H. (1986) *Never Satisfied: A History of Diets, Fantasies and Fat,* New York: Macmillan.

Selvini-Palazzoli M. S. (1985) Anorexia nervosa, a syndrome of the affluent society (transl. from Italian by V. F. Di Nicola), *Transcultural Psychiat. Res. Rev.* **22** (3): 199.

Shorter, E. (1984) *History of Women's Bodies,* London: Pelican.

Silverstein, B., Perdue, L., Peterson, B., Vogel, L. and Fantini, D. A. (1986) Possible causes of the thin standard of bodily attractiveness for women, *Int. J. Eating Disord.* **5** (5): 907–916.

Slade, P. (1982) Towards a functional analysis of anorexia nervosa and bulimia nervosa, *Br. J. Clin. Psychol.* **21**: 167–179.

Sobal, J. and Stunkard, A. (1989) Socioeconomic status and obesity: a review of the literature, *Psychol. Bull.* **105** (2): 260–275.

Sontag, S. (1978) *Illness as Metaphor,* New York: Farrar, Straus and Giroux.

Stunkard, A. (1959) Eating patterns and obesity, *Psychiat. Quart.* **33**: 284–292.

Sundgot-Borgen, J. (1993) Prevalence of eating disorders in elite female athletes, *Int. J. Sport Nutrition* **3** (1): 29–40.

Szmukler, G. (1983) Weight and food pre-occupation in a population of English school girls. In G. J. Bergman (ed.) *Understanding Anorexia Nervosa and Bulimia* – Proc. 4th Ross Conference on Medical Research, pp. 21–27, Ohio: Ross Laboratories.

Szmukler, G. I., Eisler, I., Gillies, C. and Hayward, M. E. (1985) The implications of anorexia nervosa in a ballet school, *J. Psychiat. Res.* **19** (2/3): 177–181.

Szmukler, G. I., McCance, C., McCrone, L. and Hunter, D. (1984) Anorexia nervosa: a psychiatric case register study from Aberdeen, *Psychol. Med.* **16**: 49–58.

Theander, S. (1970) Anorexia nervoda: a psychiatric investigation of 94 female patients, *Acta Psychiat. Scand. Supp.* **214**: 1–194.

Vincent, L. M. (1979) *Competing with the Sylph: Dancers and the Pursuit of the Ideal Body Form,* New York: Andrews & McMeel.

Wallechinsky, D., Wallace, I. and Wallace, A. (1977) *Book of Lists*, New York: William Morrow.

Walsh, M. (1979) The democratisation of fashion: the emergence of the women's dress pattern industry, *J. Am. Hist.* **66** (September).

Wardle, J. and Beinhart, H. (1981) Binge eating: a theoretical review, *Br. J. Clin. Psychol.* **20**: 97–109.

Weight, L. and Noakes, T. (1987) Is running an analog of anorexia? a survey of the incidence of eating disorders in female distance runners, *Medicine and Science in Sports and Exercise* **19** (3): 213–217.

Williams, P. and King, M. (1987) The epidemic of anorexia nervosa: another medical myth?, *Lancet* **i**: 205–207.

Wolf, N. (1990) *The Beauty Myth*, London: Chatto & Windus.

Wooley, O. W. and Wooley, S. C. (1982) The Beverly Hills eating disorder: the mass marketing of anorexia nervosa, *Int. J. Eating Disord.* **1**: 57–69.

Wooley, O. W., Wooley, S. C. and Dyrenforth, S. R. (1979) Obesity and women II: a neglected feminist topic, *Women Studies Int. Quart.* **2**: 81–89.

2 THE CONCEPT OF CULTURE BOUNDEDNESS AND EATING DISORDERS

Bell, I. R. (1985) *Holy Anorexia*, Chicago: The University of Chicago Press.

Berthe, G. (1909) *Historique de La Purgation*, Henri Jouve: Paris.

Budge, E. and Wallis, A. (1913) *The Syriac Book of Medicine*, vol. II, (English Translation), Oxford: Oxford University Press.

Cassidy, C. (1982) Protein-energy malnutrition as a culture bound syndrome, *Cult. Med. Psychiat.* **6**: 325.

Devereux, G. (1955) *Basic Problems of Ethnopsychiatry*, Chicago: University of Chicago Press.

Di Nicola, V. (1990) Anorexia multiform: self starvation in historical and cultural context. Part II: Anorexia nervosa as a culture reactive syndrome, *Transcultural Psychiat. Res. Rev.* **27**: 245–285.

Garrison, F. (1929) *An Introduction to the History of Medicine*, Philadelphia: W. B. Saunders.

Gilles de la Tourette, G. A. E. B. (1895) *Traité Clinique et Therapeutique de l'Hystérie*, Paris: Plou, Nourit et Co.

Gordon, R. (1990) *Anorexia and Bulimia: Anatomy of a Social Epidemic*, Cambridge, Mass.: Basil Blackwell.

Gruner, C. O. (1930) *A Treatise on the Canon of Medicine of Avicenna*, incorporating a translation of the first book, pp. 441–494. Reprinted (1970), New York: M. Keely.

Gull, W. W. (1874) Anorexia nervosa, *Trans. Clin. Soc. (London)* **7**: 22–28. Reprinted in R. M. Kaufman and M. Heinman (eds) (1964) *Evolution of Psychosomatic Concepts: Anorexia Nervosa – A Paradigm*, New York: International Universities Press.

Hahn, R. (1983) Culture-bound syndromes unbound. Presented at International Congress of Anthropology and Ethnology, Vancouver.

Hare, E. (1981) The two manias: a study of the modern concept of mania, *Br. J. Psychiat.* **138:** 89–99.

Jaspers, K. (1959) *Allgemeine Psychopathologie*, seventh edition (transl. by J. Howing and M. Hamilton, 1962), pp. 732, 742, Manchester: Manchester University Press.

Kiev, A. (1972) *Transcultural Psychiatry*, London: Penguin.

Kleinman, A. (1977) Depression, somatisation and the new cross-cultural psychiatry, *Soc. Sci. Med.* **11:** 3.

Kraepelin, E. (1904) 'Vergleichende Psychiatrie', translated as 'Comparative psychiatry', in S. Hirch and M. Shepherd (eds) (1974) *Themes and Variations in European Psychiatry*, Bristol: Wright.

Lacey, J. H. (1982) Anorexia nervosa and a bearded female saint, *Br. Med. J.* December: 18–25.

Lasègue, C. (1873) De l'anorexie hystérique, *Arch. Gen. de Med.* 385. Reprinted in R. M. Kaufman and M. Heiman (eds) (1964) *Evolution of Psychosomatic Concepts: Anorexia Nervosa: A Paradigm*, New York: International University Press.

Leff, J. (1988) *Psychiatry Around the Globe*, London: Gaskell Publications, Royal College of Psychiatrists.

Littlewood, R. (1984) The individual articulation of shared symbols, *J. Operational Psychiat.* **15:** 17.

—— (1986) Russian dolls and Chinese boxes: an anthropological approach to the implicit models of comparative psychiatry. In J. Cox (ed.) *Transcultural Psychiatry*, London: Croom Helm.

Loudon, I. S. (1980) Chlorosis, anaemia and anorexia nervosa, *Br. Med. J.* **2:** 1669–1675.

Nasser, M. (1988) Culture and weight consciousness, *J. Psychosomatic Res.* **32:** 573–577.

—— (1993) A prescription of vomiting: historical footnotes, *Int. J. Eating Disord.* **13:** 129–131.

Orbach, S. (1986) *Hunger Strike: The Anorectic's Struggle as a Metaphor for Our Age*, New York: Norton.

Prince, R. (1983) Is anorexia nervosa a culture-bound syndrome?, *Transcultural Psychiat. Res. Rev.* **20:** 299.

Rampling, D. (1985) Ascetic ideals and anorexia nervosa, *J. Psychiat. Res.* **19** (2/3): 89–94.

Raymond of Capua, *The Life of Catherine of Sienna* (transl., intro. and annotated by C. Kearns, 1980), Wilmington: Michael Glazier.

Robertson, M. (1992) *Starving in Silences: An Exploration of Anorexia Nervosa*, Sydney: Allen & Unwin.

Ritenbaugh, C. (1982) Obesity as a culture bound syndrome, *Cult. Med. Psychiat.* **6:** 347.

Russell, G. (1985) The changing nature of anorexia nervosa, *J. Psychiat. Res.* **19** (2/3): 101–109.

Swartz, L. (1985) Anorexia nervosa as a culture-bound syndrome, *J. Soc. Sci. Med.* **20** (7): 725–730.

Schwartz, D. M., Thompson, M. and Johnson, C. (1983) *Eating Disorders and Culture: Anorexia Nervosa – Recent Developments in Research*, pp. 83–84, New York: Alan R. Liss.

Taylor, D. (1985) The sick child predicament, *Aust. New Zeland J. Psychiat.* **19**: 130–137.

Yap, P. (1951) Mental diseases peculiar to certain cultures, *J. Ment. Sci.* **97**: 313–327.

3 THE EMERGENCE OF EATING DISORDERS IN OTHER CULTURES/SOCIETIES

Abou-Saleh, M., Younis, Y. and Karim, L. Anorexia nervosa in the Arab culture, *Int. J. Eating Disord.* (submitted).

Abrams, K., Allen, L. and Gray, J. (1993) Disordered eating attitudes and behaviours, psychological adjustment and ethnic identity: comparison of black and white female college students, *Int. J. Eating Disord.* **14** (1): 49–57.

Ahmad, S., Waller, G. and Verduyn, C. (1994) Eating attitudes among Asian schoolgirls: the role of perceived parental control, *Int. J. Eating Disord.* **15** (1): 91–97.

Andersen, A. and Hay, A. (1985) Racial and socioeconomic influences in anorexia nervosa and bulimia, *Int. J. Eating Disord.* **4** (4): 479–487.

Anderson, A. E. and Di Domenico, L. (1992) Diet vs shape content of popular male and female magazines: a dose-response relationship to the incidence of eating disorders, *Int. J. Eating Disord.* **11**: 283–287.

Apter, A., Shah, M., Iancu, I., Abramovitch, H., Weizman, A. and Tanyo, S. (1994) Cultural effects on eating attitudes in Israeli subpopulations and hospitalised anorectics, *Genetic Soc. Gen. Psychol. Monogr.* **120** (1): 83–99.

Azuma, Y. and Henmi, M. (1982) A study on the incidence of anorexia nervosa in school girls, *Annual Report of the Research Group into Eating Disorders, Japan*, pp. 30–34.

Bello, M. Prevalence of eating disorders in a school population in Buenos Aires, Argentina (unpublished/personal communication).

Birch, L. (1980) The effects of peer models' food choices and eating behaviours on pre-schooler's food preferences, *Child Development* **51**: 489–496.

Bruch, H. (1966) Anorexia nervosa and its differential diagnosis, *J. Nrv. Ment. Dis.* **141** (5): 555–566.

—— (1978) *The Golden Cage: The Enigma of Anorexia Nervosa*, London: Open Books.

Brumberg, J. (1988) *Fasting Girls: The Emergence of Anorexia Nervosa as a Modern Disease*, Cambridge, Mass.: Harvard University Press.

Buchan, T. and Gregory, D. (1984) Anorexia nervosa in a black Zimbabwean, *Br. J. Psychiat.* **145**: 326–330.

Buhrich, N. (1981) Frequency of presentation of anorexia nervosa in Malaysia, *Aust. New Zealand J. Psychiat.* **15**: 153–155.

Bulik, C. (1987) Eating disorders in immigrants: two case reports, *Int. J. Eating Disord.* **6** (1): 133–141.

Button, E. J. and Whitehouse, A. (1981) Subclinical anorexia nervosa, *Psychol. Med.* **11**: 509–516.

Chiodo, J. and Latimer, P. (1983) Vomiting as a learned weight control technique in Bulimia, *J. Behav. Ther. Exp. Psychiat.* **14** (2): 131–135.

Choudry, I. Y. and Mumford, D. B. (1992) A pilot study of eating disorders in Mirpur (Pakistan) using an Urdu version of the Eating Attitude Test, *Int. J. Eating Disord.* **11**: 243–251.

Clarke, K. and Palmer, R. L. (1983) Eating attitudes and neurotic symptoms in university students, *Br. J. Psychiat.* **142**: 299–304.

Cooper, P. and Fairburn, C. G. (1983) Binge eating and self induced vomiting in the community: a preliminary study, *Br. J. Psychiat.* **142**: 139–144.

Crisp, A. (1967) The possible significance of some behavioural correlates of weight and carbohydrate intake, *J. Psychosomatic Res.* **11**: 117–131.

Cullberg, J. and Engström-Lindberg, M. (1988) Prevalence and incidence of eating disorders in a suburban area, *Acta Psychiat. Scand.* **78**: 314–319.

Cuzzolaro, M. (1991) The prevalence of eating disorders in Italy. Presented at International Symposium on Eating Disorders, Paris, April.

Dolan, B. and Ford, K. (1991) Binge eating and dietary restraint: a cross cultural analysis, *Int. J. Eating Disord.* **10** (3): 345–353.

Dolan, B., Lacey, H. and Evans, C. (1990) Eating behaviours and attitudes to weight and shape in British women from three ethnic groups, *Br. J. Psychiat.* **157**: 523–528.

Edwards, W. (1989) *Modern Japan through its Weddings: Gender, Person and Society in Ritual Portrayal*, Stanford, Calif.: Stanford University Press.

Eisler, I. and Szmukler, G. (1985) Social class as a confounding variable in the Eating Attitude Test, *J. Psychiat. Res.* **19** (23): 171–176.

El-Islam, F., Malasi, T. and Abu-Dagga, S. (1988) Interparental differences in attitudes and cultural changes in Kuwait, *Soc. Psychiat. Psychiat. Epidemiol.* **23**: 109–113.

El Sarrag, M. E. (1968) Psychiatry in Northern Sudan: a study in comparative psychiatry, *Br. J. Psychiat.* **114**: 946–948.

Emmons, L. (1992) 'Dieting and purging behaviour in black and white high school students', *J. Am. Dietetic Assoc.* **92** (3): 306–312.

Faltus, F. (1986) Anorexia nervosa in Czechoslovakia, *Int. J. Eating Disord.* **3** (5): 581–585.

Famuyiwa, O. (1988) Anorexia nervosa in two Nigerians, *Acta Psychiat. Scand.* **78**: 550–554.

Fichter, M., Elton, M., Sourdi, S., Weyerer, S., Koptagel-Ilal, G. (1988) Anorexia nervosa in Greek and Turkish adolescents, *Eur. Arch. Psychiat. Neurolog. Sci.* **237**: 200–208.

Fichter, M. M., Weyerer, S., Sourdi, L. and Sourdi, Z. (1983) The epidemiology of anorexia nervosa: a comparison of Greek adolescents living in Germany and Greek adolescents living in Greece. In P. L. Darby, P. M. Garfinkel, D. M. Garner and D. V. Coscina (eds) *Anorexia Nervosa: Recent Developments in Research*, pp. 95–105, New York: Liss.

Ford, C. S. and Beach, F. A. (1952) *Patterns of Sexual Behaviour*, New York: Ace Books.

Ford, K., Dolan, B. and Evans, C. (1990) Cultural factors in the aetiology of eating disorders: evidence from body shape preference of Arab students, *J. Psychosomatic Res.* **34** (5): 501–507.

Furnham, A. C. and Alibhai, N. (1983) Cross cultural differences in the perception of female body shapes, *Psychol. Med.* **13**: 829–837.

Garner, D. M., Garfinkel, P. E., Schwartz, D. and Thompson, M. (1980) Cultural expectations of thinness in women, *Psychiat. Rep.* **47**: 483–491.

Goldberg, D. and Huxley, P. (1980) *Mental Illness in the Community*, London: Tavistock.

Goldblatt, P. B., Moore, M. E. and Stunkard, A. J. (1965) Social factors in obesity, *J. Am. Med. Assoc.* **192**: 97–102.

Grant, L. (1994) Why Fay does not want to look like Naomi: why dieting is a black and white issue, *Independent on Sunday*, 25 September, London.

Gray, J., Ford, K. and Kelly, L. (1987) The prevalence of bulimia in a black college population, *Int. J. Eating Disord.* **6**: 733–740.

Gruner, C. O. (1930) *A Treatise on the Canon of Medicine of Avicenna*, incorporating a translation of the first book, pp. 441–499. Reprinted (1970), New York: M. Keely.

Gustavson, C., Pumariega, A., Gustavson, J., Herrara-Amighetti, L., Pate, J., Hester, C. and Gabaldon, M. (1993) Body image distortion among male and female American and Costa Rican students and female Japanese students, *Perceptual and Motor Skills* **76**: 127–130.

Hamadi, S. (1960) *The Temperament and Character of the Arabs*, Boston: Twayne Publishers.

Hassan, M. (1995) 'Psychodynamic patterns of Egyptian families of asthmatic children', MD Thesis, Alexandria University, Egypt.

Hawkins, R. and Clement, P. (1980) Development and construct validation of a self report measure of binge eating tendencies, *Addictive Behaviours* **3**: 219–226.

Hoek, H., Bartelds, A., Bosveld, J., van der Graaf, Y., Limpens, V., Maiwald, M. and Spaaij, M. (1995) Impact of urbanisation on detection rates of eating disorders, *Am. J. Psychiat.* **152** (9): 1272–1285.

Holden, N. and Robinson, P. (1988) Anorexia nervosa and bulimia nervosa in British Blacks, *Br. J. Psychiat.* **152**: 544–549.

Hooper, M. S. and Garner, D. M. (1986) Application of the eating disorders inventory to a sample of black, white and mixed race schoolgirls in Zimbabwe, *Int. J. Eating Disord.* **5** (1): 161–168.

Hsu, L. K. G. (1987) Are eating disorders becoming more common in Blacks?, *Int. J. Eating Disord.* **6**: 113–124.

Irving, L. (1990) Mirror images effects of the standard of beauty on the self and body esteem of women exhibiting varying levels of bulimic symptoms, *J. Soc. Clin. Psychol.* **9**: 230–242.

Joergensen, J. (1992) The epidemiology of eating disorders in Fyn country, Denmark, 1977–1986, *Acta Psychiat. Scand.* **85** (1): 30–34.

Johnson-Sabine, E., Wood, K., Patton, G., Mann, A. and Wakeling, A. (1988) Abnormal eating attitudes in London school girls: a prospective epidemiological study; factors associated with abnormal response on screening questionnaires, *Psychol. Med.* **18:** 615–622.

Jones, D. J., Fox, M. M., Babigan, H. M. and Hutton, H. E. (1980) Epidemiology of anorexia nervosa in Monroe County, New York: 1960–1967, *Psychosomatic Med.* **42:** 551–558.

Kaffman, M. and Sadeh, T. (1989) Anorexia nervosa in the Kibbutz: factors influencing the development of monoideistic fixation, *Int. J. Eating Disord.* **8** (1): 33–53.

Kamata, K., Nogami, Y. and Momma, K. (1987) Binge eating among female students, *Jpn. J. Psychiat. Neurol.* **41** (1): 151–152.

King, M. B. (1986) Eating disorders in General Practice, *Br. Med. J.* **293:** 1412–1414.

—— (1989) Eating disorders in general practice population: prevalence, characteristics and follow up at 12–18 months, *Psychol. Med. Monogr.* Suppl. **14:** 134.

King, M. B. and Bhugra, D. (1989) Eating disorders: lessons from a cross-cultural study, *Psychol. Med.* **19:** 955–958.

Kope, T. M. and Sack, W. H. (1987) Anorexia nervosa in South East Asian refugees: a report on three cases, *J. Am. Acad. Child Adolesc. Psychiat.* **26** (5): 795–797.

Krch, F. (1994) Needs and possibilities of prevention of eating disorders in the Czech republic. Presented at IV International Conference on Eating Disorders, New York.

—— (1995) Obesity in the Czech Republic: fear of obesity as one of the important risk factors in the onset and development of eating disorders. Presented at the European Council of Eating Disorders (ECED) September 1995, Dublin.

Lacey, H. and Dolan, B. (1988) Bulimia in British Blacks and Asians: a catchment area study, *Br. J. Psychiat.* **152:** 73–79.

Lasègue, C. (1873) De l'anorexie hystérique, *Arch. Gen. de Med.* 385. Reprinted in R. M. Kaufman and M. Heinman (eds) *Evolution of Psychosomatic Concepts: Anorexia Nervosa, a Paradigm* (1964) New York: International University Press.

Lawrence, M. (1987) *Fed up and Hungry: Women, Oppression and Food*, London: The Women's Press.

Ledoux, S., Choquet, M. and Flament, M. (1991) Eating disorders among adolescents in unselected French population, *Int. J. Eating Disord.* **10:** 81–89.

Lee, S., Chiu, H. F. K. and Chen, C. (1989) Anorexia nervosa in Hong Kong: why not more in Chinese?, *Br. J. Psychiat.* **154:** 683–685.

Lee, S., Hsu, G. and Wing, Y. (1992) Bulimia nervosa in Hong Kong Chinese patients, *Br. J. Psychiat.* **161:** 545–551.

Leff, J. (1988) *Psychiatry Round the Globe*, Gaskell Psychiatry Series, London: The Royal College of Psychiatrists.

Lewnes, A. (1991) Fat chance: Cairo fitness centres surveyed, *Cairo Today* **31** (1): 106–110.

Lucas, A. R., Beard, C. M., O'Fallon, W. M. and Kurland, L. T. (1988) Anorexia nervosa in Rochester Minnesota: a 45-year study, *Mayo Clinics Proc.* **63:** 433–442.

Lucero, K., Hicks, R., Bramlette, J., Brassington, G. and Welter, M. (1992) Frequency of eating problems among Asian and Caucasian college women, *Psychol. Rep.* **71**: 255–258.

Mangweth, B., Harrison, P. and Hudson, J. (1994) Bulimia nervosa in two cultures: a comparison of Austrian and American college students. Presented at VI International Congress on Eating Disorders, New York, May.

Mann, A. H., Wakeling, A., Wood, K., Monck, E., Dobbs, R. and Szmukler, G. (1983) Screening for abnormal eating attitudes and psychiatric morbidity in an unselected population of 15 year old school girls, *Psychol. Med.* **13**: 573–580.

Marie Claire (1995) Russia's millionaire children, spoilt by their new-found wealth. October.

Martin, J. and Wollitzer, A. (1988) The prevalence, secrecy and psychology of purging in a family practice setting, *Int. J. Eating Disord.* **7**: 315–319.

McCourt, J. and Waller, G. (1995) Developmental role of perceived parental control in eating psychopathology of Asian and Caucasian school girls, *Int. J. Eating Disord.* **17**: 277–282.

Minuchin, S., Rossman, B. and Baker, L. (1978) *Psychosomatic Families: Anorexia Nervosa in Context*, Cambridge Mass.: Harvard University Press.

Mukai, T., Crago, M. and Shisslak, K. (1994) Eating attitudes and weight preoccupation among female high school students in Japan, *J. Child Psychol. Psychiat.* **33** (4): 677–688.

Mumford, D. B. and Whitehouse, A. M. (1988) 'Increased prevalence of bulimia nervosa among Asian school girls', *Br. Med. J.* **297**: 718.

Mumford, D. B., Whitehouse, A. M. and Choudry, I. (1992) Survey of eating disorders in English-medium Schools in Lahore, Pakistan, *Int. J. Eating Disord.* **11** (2): 173-184.

Mumford, D. B., Whitehouse, A. M. and Platts, M. (1991) Socio-cultural correlates of eating disorders among Asian school girls in Bradford, *Br. J. Psychiat.* **158**: 222–228.

Murphy, R. (1993) The effects of observing male and female photographic models on men and women's self-esteem and body image. Presented at British Psychological Society Conference, Blackpool, UK, April.

Nakane, A. and Umino, M. (1987) Psychotherapy of anorexia nervosa in young adolescence, *Jpn. J. Psychiat. Neurol.* **41** (1): 153.

Nasser, M. (1984) A comparative study of the prevalence of anorexia nervosa and abnormal eating attitudes among Arab female students of both London and Cairo Universities, M.Phil Thesis, London University.

—— (1986) Comparative study of the prevalence of abnormal eating attitudes among Arab female students at both London and Cairo Universities, *Psychol. Med.* **16**: 621–625.

—— (1988) Culture and weight consciousness, *J. Psychosomatic Res.* **32**: 573–577.

—— (1992) Screening for abnormal eating attitudes in a population of Egyptian secondary school girls, Doctor of Medicine (DM) Thesis, Southampton University, UK.

—— (1994a) The psychometric properties of the eating attitudes test in a non-western population, *Soc. Psychiat. Psychiat. Epidemiol.* **29:** 88–94.

—— (1994b) Screening for abnormal eating attitudes in a population of Egyptian secondary school girls, *Soc. Psychiat. Psychiat. Epidemiol.* **29:** 88–94.

Nasser, M. and Abrams, K. Western/Non Western . . . similar/dissimilar: a pilot study, *Soc. Psychiat. Psychiat. Epidemiol.* (submitted).

Neumärker, U., Dudeck, U., Vollrath, M., Neumärker, K. and Steinhausen, H. (1992) Eating attitudes among adolescent anorexia nervosa patients and normal subjects in former West and East Berlin: a transcultural comparison, *Int. J. Eating Disord.* **12** (3): 281–289.

Nogami, Y., Yamaguchi, T. and Ishiwata, H. (1984) The prevalence of binge eating in the Japanese university and high school population. Presented at the International Conference of Eating Disorders, Swansea, UK.

Nunes, M., Bagatini, L. and Salvador, C. (1991) What to think of anorexia nervosa in Brazil, a country of hunger and undernourishment? Poster presentation at the International Symposium on Eating Disorders, Paris, April.

Nwaefuna, A. (1981) Anorexia nervosa in a developing country, *Br. J. Psychiat.* **138:** 270–271.

Ohzeki, T., Hanaki, K., Motozumi, H., Ishitani, N., Matsuda-Ohtahara, H., Sunaguchi, M. and Shiraki, K. (1990) Prevalence of obesity, leanness and anorexia nervosa in Japanese boys and girls aged 12–14 years, *Ann. Nutrition and Metabolism* **34:** 208–212.

Okasha, A., Kamel, M., Sadek, A., Loatif, F. and Bishry, F. (1977) Psychiatric morbidity among university students in Egypt, *Br. J. Psychiat.* **131:** 149–154.

Ong, Y. L., Tsoi, W. F. and Cheah, J. S. (1982) A clinical and psychosocial study of seven cases of anorexia nervosa in Singapore, *Singapore Med. J.* **23:** 255–261.

Oyewumi, L. and Kazarian, S. (1992) Abnormal eating attitudes among a group of Nigerian Youth: 1, Bulimic behaviour, *East African Med. J.* **69** (12): 663–666.

Parekh, B. (1983) Asians in Britain – problems or opportunity. In *Five Views of Multiracial Britain*. London: Commission for Social Equality by special arrangement with BBC Television Further Education.

Pate, J., Pumariega, A., Hester, C. and Garner, D. (1992) Cross-cultural patterns in eating disorders: a review, *J. Am. Acad. Child Adolesc. Psychiat.* **31** (5): 802–809.

Pumariega, J., Edwards, P. and Mitchell, C. (1984) Anorexia nervosa in black adolescents, *J. Am. Acad. Child Adolesc. Psychiat.* **23:** 111–114.

—— (1986) Acculturation and eating attitudes in adolescent girls, a comparative and correlational study, *J. Am. Acad. Child Adolesc. Psychiat.* **25** (2): 276–279.

Pumarino, H. and Vivanco, N. (1982) Anorexia nervosa: medical and psychiatric characteristics of 30 patients, *Revista Medica de Chile,* **110:** 1081–1092.

Raich, R. M., Resen, J. C., Deus, J., Perez, O., Requena, A. and Gross, J. (1992) Eating disorders symptoms among adolescents in the USA and Spain: a comparative study, *Int. J. Eating Disord.* **11**: 63–72.

Rathner, G. and Messner, K. (1993) Detection of eating disorders in a small rural town: an epidemiological study, *Psychol. Med.* **23**: 175–184.

Rathner, G., Túry, F., Szabo, P., Geyer, M., Rumpold, G., Forgaces, A., Söllner, W. and Plöttner, G. (1995) Prevalence of eating disorders and minor psychiatric morbidity in Central Europe before the political changes in 1989: a cross-cultural study, *Psychol. Med.* **25**: 1027–1035.

Reiss, D. (1996) Abnormal eating attitudes and behaviours in two ethnic groups from a female British urban population, *Psychol. Med.* **26**: 289–299.

Robertson, M. (1992) *Starving in Silences: An Exploration of Anorexia Nervosa*, Sydney: Allen & Unwin.

Robinson, P. and Andersen, A. (1985) Anorexia nervosa in American Blacks, *J. Psychiat. Res.* **19** (2/3): 183–188.

Roden, C. (1989) *Mediterranean Cookery*, London: BBC Books.

Rosen, C., Shaffer, C., Dummer, G., Cross, L., Deuman, G. and Malmberg, S. (1988) Prevalence of pathogenic weight control behaviours among native American women and girls, *Int. J. Eating Disord.* **7** (6): 807–811.

Rowland, C. (1970) Anorexia and obesity, *Int. Psychiat. Clinics* **7**: 37–137.

Ruderman, A. (1985) Dysphoric mood and overeating: a test of restraints disinhibition hypothesis, *J. Abnorm. Psychol.* **94**: 78–85.

Rudofsky, B. (1972) *The Unfashionable Human Body*, New York: Doubleday.

Russell, G. (1985) The changing nature of anorexia nervosa, *J. Psychiat. Res.* **19** (2/3): 101–109.

Schmidt, U. (1993) Bulimia nervosa in the Chinese, *Int. J. Eating Disord.* **14** (4): 505–509.

Schwartz, H. (1986) *Never Satisfied: A Cultural History of Diets, Fantasies and Fat*, New York: Macmillan.

Selvini-Pallazoli, M. (1974) *Self Starvation: From Individual to Family Therapy in the Treatment of Anorexia Nervosa* (transl. by A. Pomerans), New York: Jason Aronson.

—— (1985) Anorexia nervosa: a syndrome of the affluent society, *Transcultural Psychiat. Res. Rev.* **22**: 199–205.

Silber, T. (1986) Anorexia nervosa in Blacks and Hispanics, *Int. J. Eating Disord.* **5**: 121–128.

Silverstein, B., Perdue, L., Peterson, B. and Kelly, E. (1986) The role of the mass media in promoting a thin standard of bodily attractiveness for women, *Sex Roles* **14**: 519–532.

Smith, J. and Krejci, J. (1991) Minorities join the majority: eating disturbance among Hispanics and native American youth, *Int. J. Eating Disord.* **10** (2): 179–186.

Steinhausen, H. C. (1984) Transcultural comparison of eating attitudes in young females and anorectic patients, *Eur. Arch. Psychiat. Neurol. Sci.* **234**: 198–201.

Steinhausen, H. C., Neumärker, K., Vollrath, M., Dudeck, U. and Neu-märker, U. (1992) A transcultural comparison of the Eating Disorder Inventory in former East and West Berlin, *Int. J. Eating Disord.* **12** (4): 407–416.

Strauss, J., Levy, C., Kreipe, R. (1994) Body norms, satisfaction and cul-tural pressures in African-American and white women. Presented at the VI International Congress on Eating Disorders, New York, May.

Stunkard, A. (1959) Eating patterns and obesity, *Psychiat. Quart.* **33**: 284–292.

Suematsu, H., Ishikawa, H., Kuboki, T. and Ito, T. (1985) Statistical studies of anorexia nervosa in Japan, detailed clinical data on 1,011 patients, *Psychotherapy and Psychosomatics* **43**: 96–103.

Szabo, P. and Túry, F. (1991) The prevalence of bulimia nervosa in a Hungarian college and secondary school population, *Psychotherapy and Psychosomatics* **56**: 43–47.

Szmukler, G. (1983) Weight and food pre-occupation in a population of English school girls. In G. J. Bergman (ed.) *Understanding Anorexia Nervosa and Bulimia*, 4th Ross Conference on Medical Research, pp. 21–27, Ohio: Ross Laboratories.

Szmukler, G., McCance, C., McCrone, L. and Hunter, D. (1984) Anor-exia nervosa: a psychiatric case register study from Aberdeen, *Psychol. Med.* **16**: 49–58.

Takahashi, S., Arata, O., Yukiko, M., Toshihide, N. and Totsuka, S. (1991) Eating attitudes and parental bonding in Japanese young women. Presented at the International Symposium on Eating Disor-ders, Paris.

Takagi, S., Nishizono-Maher, A. and Asai, M. (1991) Study of predispos-ing factors and initiating factors of eating disorders in Japan. Presented at the International Symposium on Eating Disorders, Paris, April.

Theander, S. (1970) Anorexia nervosa: a psychiatric investigation of 94 female patients, *Acta. Psychiat. Scand.* Suppl. **214**: 1–194.

Thomas, J. and Szmukler, G. I. (1985) Anorexia nervosa in patients of Afro-Caribbean extraction, *Br. J. Psychiat.* **146**: 653–656.

Tordjman, S., Zittoun, C., Anderson, G., Flament, M. and Jeammet, P. (1994) Preliminary study of eating disorders among French female ado-lescents and young adults, *Int. J. Eating Disord.* **16** (3): 301–305.

Toriola, A., Dolan, B. and Evans, C. Intergenerational and cross-cultural influences on the weight satisfaction of Nigerian women in Nigeria and Britain (unpublished).

Turpin, C. (1995) Social class, culture and eating disorders: a comparison between two schools in Cairo, Egypt [French]. University René Des-cartes, Paris.

Van Den Brouke, S. and Vandereycken, W. (1986) Risk factors for the development of eating disorders in adolescent exchange students: an exploratory survey, *J. Adolesc.* **9**: 145–150.

Waadegaard, M. and Petersson, B. (1995) Occurrence of bulimic beha-viour among a group of Danish Medical students [Danish], *Ugeskr Laeger* **12**, 157 (24): 3468–3472.

Waller, G., Hamilton, K. and Shaw, J. (1992) Media influences on body size estimation in eating disordered and comparison women, *Br. Rev. Bulimia Anorexia Nervosa* **6**: 81–87.

Wardle, J. and Beinhart, H. (1981) Binge eating: a theoretical review, *Br. J. Clin. Psychol.* **20**: 97–109.

Włodarczyk-Bisaga, K. (1994) Pattern of response to the eating attitude test (EAT-26) among Polish adolescent females. Presented at the VI International Conference on Eating Disorders, New York, May.

Willi, J. and Grossman, S. (1983) Epidemiology of anorexia nervosa in a defined region of Switzerland, *Am. J. Psychiat.* **140**: 564–567.

Willi, J., Giacometti, G. and Limacher, B. (1990) Update on the epidemiology of anorexia nervosa in a defined region of Switzerland, *Am. J. Psychiat.* **147** (11): 154–157.

Williams, P. and King, M. (1987) The epidemic of anorexia nervosa: another medical myth?, *Lancet* (1): 205–207.

Worsley, A. (1981) In the eye of the beholder: social and personal characteristics of teenagers and their impressions of themselves and fat and slim people, *Br. J. Med. Psychol.* **54**: 231–242.

Yates, A. (1989) Current perspectives on eating disorders: 1 history, psychological and biological aspects, *J. Am. Acad. Child Adolesc. Psychiat.* **29** (1): 1–9.

Zukerfeld, R. and Cormillot, A. (1991) Eating disorders in obese women in Buenos Aires. Presented at the International Symposium on Eating Disorders, Paris, April.

4 THE OTHER WOMEN – IMMUNE OR VULNERABLE?

Amin, Q. (1899) *Tahrir el Mar'aa* (Women's Emancipation) [Arabic], Cairo.

—— (1901) *El-Mar'aa El-gadida* (New Woman) [Arabic], Cairo.

Baykan, A. (1990) Women between fundamentalism and modernity. In B. S. Turner (ed.) *Theories of Modernity and Post-modernity*, London: Sage.

Becker, W. A. (1866) *Charicles or Illustrations of the Private Life of the Greeks* (transl. by F. Metcalfe), London.

Bennett, W. and Gurin, J. (1982) *The Dieter's Dilemma: Eating Less and Weighing More*, New York: Basic Books.

Boskind-Lodahl, M. (1976) Cinderella's step sisters: a feminist perspective on anorexia nervosa and bulimia, *J. Women in Culture and Society* **2**: 342–356.

Bruch, H. (1978) *The Golden Cage: the Enigma of Anorexia Nervosa*, Cambridge, Mass.: Harvard University Press.

—— (1988) *Conversations with Anorexics*, New York: Basic Books.

Brumberg, J. (1988) *Fasting Girls: The Emergence of Anorexia Nervosa as a Modern Disease*, Cambridge, Mass.: Harvard University Press.

Burton, R. (1954) *The Arabian Nights*, Pocket Books, NT.

Campbell, J. (1962) *Oriental Mythology*, New York: Viking.

Catina, A. (1995) Young women in East and West of Europe: social ideals and eating disorders. Presented at The European Council of Eating Disorders (ECED), September 1995, Dublin.

Chernin, K. (1981) The mysterious case of Ellen West. In *The Obsession: Reflections on the Tyranny of Slenderness*, New York: Harper and Row.

—— (1986) *The Hungry Self: Women: Eating and Identity*, London: Virago.

Clark, K. (1980) *Feminine Beauty*, London: Weidenfeld and Nicolson.

Corin, C. (1992) *Superwoman and the Double Burden: Women's Experience of Change in Central and Eastern Europe and the Former Soviet Union*. London: Scarlet Press.

Crisp, A. H. (1977) Diagnosis and outcome of anorexia nervosa: the St George's View, *Proc. Roy. Soc. Med.* **70**: 464–470.

Darwish, A. (1994) Egypt's rulers divided over schoolgirl veils, *The Independent*, 8 August, London.

De Beauvoir, S. (1972) *The Second Sex*, London: Penguin.

De Riencourt, A. (1983) *Woman and Power in History*, London: Honeyglen Publishing.

Di Nichola, V. F. (1988a) Anorexia nervosa from a transcultural perspective: the requirements for a comprehensive model, *The BASH Magazine* **7** (9): 210–215.

—— (1988b) Essay-review of Susi Orbach's 'Hunger Strike: The Anorectic's Struggle as a Metaphor for Our Age', *Transcultural Res. Rev.* **25** (1): 47–54.

Dill, S. (1925) *Roman Society from Nero to Marcus*, London: Aurelius.

Dolan, B. (1994) Why women? Gender issues and eating disorders, Introduction. In B. Dolan and I. Gitzinger (eds) *Why Women? Gender Issues and Eating Disorders*, London: The Athlone Press.

Dubois, J. A. (1928) *Hindu Manners, Customs and Ceremonies* (transl. by H. K. Beauchamp), Oxford: Clarendon Press.

Duff-Gordon, L. (1969) *Letters from Egypt (1862–1869)*. Reprinted, London: Routledge and Kegan Paul.

Duke, B. (1985) *Compañeras: Women, Art and Social Change in Latin America*, San Francisco: City Light Books.

Edwards, W. (1989) *Modern Japan through its Weddings: Gender, Person and Society in Ritual Portrayal*, Stanford, Calif.: Stanford University Press.

El-Ashmawi, S. (1994) Compulsory hijab (veiling) is religiously illegal [Arabic], *Rose El-Youssef*, No 3454, 22–28, 28–31.

El-Bokhary, A. (1868) *Kitab el Gami el Sahib* (the book of Mohammed's sayings in Arabic).

El-Saadawi (1980) *The Hidden Face of Eve, Women in the Arab World* (transl. by Dr Sherif Hetata), London: Zed Press.

Feierabed, R., Feierabed, I. and Sleet, D. (1973) Need achievement, coerciveness of government and political unrest: a cross national analysis, *J. Cross Cult. Psychol.* **4** (3): 314–323.

Gary, B. and Jones, B. (1987) Psychotherapy and black women, *A survey of the National Medical Association* **79**: 177–181.

Gordon, R. (1990) *Anorexia and Bulimia: Anatomy of a Social Epidemic*, Cambridge, Mass.: Basil Blackwell.

Gull, W. (1868) The Address in Medicine delivered before the annual meeting of the BMA at Oxford, *Lancet* **2:** 171.

Hijab, N. (1988) *Women Power: The Arab Debate on Women at Work*, Cambridge: Cambridge University Press.

hooks, b. (1981) *Ain't I a Woman: Black Women and Feminism*, London: Pluto Press.

Hugo, V. (1964) *Les Orientales en Oeuvres Poetiques*, ed. Pierre Albany, Paris: Gallimard.

Ionesco, E. (1962) *Rhinoceros, The Chairs and The Lesson*, London: Penguin Plays.

Joughin, N., Crisp, A. and Humphrey, H. (1991) Religious belief and anorexia nervosa. Presented at the International Symposium on Eating Disorders, April, Paris.

Kabbani, R. (1986) *Europe's Myth of the Orient: Devise and Rule*, Bloomington: Indiana University Press.

Kaffman, M. and Sadeh, T. (1989) Anorexia nervosa in the kibbutz: factors influencing the development of monoideisic fixation, *Int. J. Eating Disord.* **8** (1): 33–53.

Kahlo, F. (1995) *Diary of Frida Kahlo: an Intimate Self-portrait* (with an introduction by Carlos Fuentes), London: Bloomsbury.

Karnouk, L. (1988) *Modern Egyptian Art: The Emergence of a National Style*, Cairo: The American University Press.

Lane, E. (1890) *An Account of the Manners and Customs of Modern Egyptians* (1833–35), Cairo: Livre de France.

Leon, D. (1969) *The Kibbutz: A New Way of Life*, London: Pergamon.

Lewis, L. and Johnson, C. (1985) A comparison of sex roles orientation between bulimia and normal controls, *Int. J. Eating Disord.* **4:** 247–257.

Lutfi El Said-Marsot, A. (1977) *Egypt's Liberal Experiment 1922–1936*, Berkeley: University of California Press.

—— (1978) The revolutionary gentlewomen in Egypt. In L. Beck and N. Keddile (eds) *Women in the Muslim World*, Cambridge, Mass.: Harvard University Press.

MacLeod, A. (1991) *Accommodating Protest: Working Women, the New Veiling and Change in Cairo*, New York: Columbia University Press.

MacLeod, S. (1981) *The Art of Starvation*, London: Virago.

Mahowald, M. (1992) To be or not to be a woman: anorexia nervosa, normative gender roles and feminism, *J. Med. and Philosophy* **17:** 233–251.

Mays, V. M. (1985) Black women working together: diversity in the same sex-relationship, *Women's Studies Int. Forum* **8:** 67–71.

Meir, G. (1975) *My Life*, London: Futura.

Meman, B. (1995) *Women's Orients: English Women and the Middle East, Sexuality, Religion and Work 1718–1981*, London: Macmillan.

Mogul, S. (1980) Asceticism in adolescence and anorexia nervosa, *Psychoanal. Study Child* **35:** 155–175.

Montagu, A. and Loring-Brace, C. (1977) *The Human Revolution*, New York: Macmillan.

Moravia, A. (1985) *1934* (transl. from the Italian by William Weaver), London: Panther Books.

Mostyn, T. (1989) *Egypt's Belle Epoque, Cairo 1869–1952*, London: Quartet.

Murase, T. (1974) Naikan therapy. In Taki Sugiyama Lebra and William Lebra (eds) *Japanese Culture and Behaviour: Selected Readings*, Honolulu: University Press of Hawaii.

Nasser, M. (1992) 'Screening for abnormal eating attitudes in a population of Egyptian secondary schoolgirls', Doctor of Medicine Thesis (DM), Southampton University, UK.

—— (1993) *Homom El-Mar'aa* (Women's Psychological Concerns) [Arabic], Cairo: Madbouli Press.

Neki, J. (1973) Psychiatry in South East Asia, *Br. J. Psychiat.* **123:** 257–269.

Nightingale, F. (1854) *Letters from Egypt: Journey on the Nile 1849–1850*, London: Barrie and Jenkins.

Orbach, S. (1978) *Fat is a Feminist Issue*, London: Paddington Press.

—— (1986) *Hunger Strike: the Anorectic's Struggle as a Metaphor for our Age*, New York: Norton.

Ortner, S. (1974) Is female to male as nature to culture?. In M. Zimbalist Rosaldo and L. Lamphore (eds) *Women, Culture and Society*, pp. 67–87, Stanford, Calif.: Stanford University Press.

Paglia, C. (1990) *Sexual Personae: Art and Decadence from Nefertiti to Emily Dixon*, London: Penguin.

Posadskaya, A. (1994) A feminist critique of policy, legislation and social consciousness in post-socialist Russia. In *Women in Russia*, London: Verso.

The Qur'an (transl. by N. G. Daood, 1956), London: Penguin.

Roberts, J. (1985) *The Triumph of the West*, London: British Broadcasting Corporation.

Robins, G. (1993) *Women in Ancient Egypt*, London: British Museum Publications.

Rose, W., Neuhaus, M. and Florin, T. (1982) Bulimia nervosa: Sex role attitude, sex role behaviour and sex role related locus of controlling bulimarexic women, *J. Psychosomatic Res.* **26** (40): 403–408.

Rousseau, J. J. (1960) Letter to M. d'Alembert on the Theatre, In *Politics and the Arts* (transl. by Allan Bloom), New York: Glencoe.

Rugh, A. (1987) *Reveal and Conceal: Dress in Contemporary Egypt*, Cairo: The American University in Cairo Press.

Russell, G. (1985) The changing nature of anorexia nervosa, *J. Psychiat. Res.* **19** (2/3): 101–109.

Said, E. (1978) *Orientalism*, London: Routledge and Kegan Paul.

Saso, M. (1990) *Women in the Japanese Working Place*, London: Hilary Shipman.

Schwartz, H. (1986) *Never Satisfied: A Cultural History of Diets, Fantasies and Fat*, New York: Macmillan.

Selvini-Pallazoli, M. (1974) *Self Starvation: From Individual to Family Therapy in the Treatment of Anorexia Nervosa* (transl. by A. Pomerans), second edition, New York: Jason Aronson.

—— (1985) Anorexia nervosa: a syndrome of the affluent society (transl. by V. F. Di Nicola), *Transcultural Psychiat. Res. Rev.* **22** (3): 199–205.

Shaarawi, H. (1986) *Harem Years – The Memoires of an Egyptian Feminist (1879–1924)* (transl. ed. and intr. by Margot Badran), London: Virago.

Sitnick, T. and Katz, J. (1984) Sex role identity and anorexia nervosa, *Int. J. Eating Disord.* **3**: 81–89.

Steiner-Adair, C. (1986) The body politic: normal female adolescent and the development of eating disorders, *J. Am. Acad. Psychoanal.* **14**: 95–114.

Stokes, M. (1994) Turkish arabesk and the city: urban popular culture as spatial practice. In A. Ahmed and D. Hastings (eds) *Islam, Globalisation and Postmodernity*, London: Routledge.

Sullivan, E. (1987) *Women in Egyptian Public Life*, Cairo: The American University in Cairo Press.

Tiger, L. and Shepher, J. (1977) *Women in the Kibbutz*, London: Penguin.

Timko, C., Striegel-Moore, R., Silberstein, L. and Rodin, J. (1987) Femininity/masculinity and disordered eating in women: how are they related?, *Int. J. Eating Disord.* **6**: 701–712.

Thornton, L. (1985) *The Orientalists, vol. 3: Women Portrayed in Orientalist Paintings*, ACR, Paris: International Courbevoie.

Tucker, J. (1986) *Women in Nineteenth Century Egypt*, Cairo: The American University in Cairo Press.

Visram, R. (1992) *Women in India and Pakistan: The Struggle for Independence from British Rule*, Cambridge: Cambridge University Press.

Watson, H. (1994) Women and the veil, personal responses to global processes. In A. Ahmed and D. Hastings (eds) *Islam, Globalisation and Postmodernity*, London: Routledge.

Weber, M. (1951) *The Religion of China*, New York: Glencoe.

Weeda-Mannak, W., Arondeus, J. and Talken, R. (1990) Sex role identity and anorexia nervosa. In J. Drenth, J. Seargant and R. Taken (eds) *European Perspectives in Psychology, vol. 3*, Chichester: Wiley.

Williams, J. (1980) Veiling in Egypt as a political and social phenomenon. In *Islam and Development*, Syracuse, N.Y.: Syracuse University Press.

Wolf, N. (1990) *The Beauty Myth*, London: Chatto & Windus.

Wooley, S. and Wooley, O. (1984) Feeling fat in a thin society, *Glamour*, pp. 198–252.

Yedlin, T. (1978) *Women in Eastern Europe and the Soviet Union*, New York: Praeger.

5 CULTURE: BETWEEN DIFFERENCES AND COMMONALITIES

Bernal, M. (1987) *Black Athena: The Afroasiatic Roots of Classical Civilisation*, London: Vintage,

Fernando, S. (1988) *Race and Culture in Psychiatry*. London: Tavistock/Routledge.

Hourani, A. (1991) *A History of Arab Peoples*, London: Faber & Faber.

Hutton, W. (1995) *The State We're In*, London: Jonathan Cape.

Nasser, M. (1994) The vague vocabulary of transcultural research, *Transcultural Psychiat. Res. Rev.* (letter to the editor) **31**: 85–88.

Palmer, R. (1979) The dietary chaos syndrome: a useful new term?, *Br. J. Med. Psychol.* **52**: 187–190.

Said, E. (1994) *Culture and Imperialism*, London: Vintage.

Schwarz, H. (1986) *Never Satisfied: a Cultural History of Diets, Fantasies and Fat*, New York: Macmillan.

Weiss, A. (1994) Changes for Muslim women in a postmodern world. In A. Ahmed and D. Hastings (eds) *Islam, Globalisation and Postmodernity*, London: Routledge.

Index